HUMAN KINETICS WEB RESOURCE

How to access the supplemental web resource

We are pleased to provide access to a web resource that supplements your *Meeting Physical Education Standards Through Meaningful Assessment*. This resource offers sample assessments and assessment templates.

Accessing the web resource is easy!
Follow these steps if you purchased a new book:

1. Visit www.HumanKinetics.com/ MeetingPhysicalEducationStandardsThroughMeaningfulAssessment.

2. Click the <u>first edition</u> link next to the book cover.

3. Click the Sign In link on the left or top of the page. If you do not have an account with Human Kinetics, you will be prompted to create one.

4. If the online product you purchased does not appear in the Ancillary Items box on the left of the page, click the Enter Key Code option in that box. Enter the key code that is printed at the right, including all hyphens. Click the Submit button to unlock your online product.

5. After you have entered your key code the first time, you will never have to enter it again to access this product. Once unlocked, a link to your product will permanently appear in the menu on the left. For future visits, all you need to do is sign in to the book's website and follow the link that appears in the left menu!

→ Click the Need Help? button on the book's website if you need assistance along the way.

How to access the web resource if you purchased a used book:

You may purchase access to the web resource by visiting the text's website, **www.HumanKinetics.com/ MeetingPhysicalEducationStandardsThroughMeaningfulAssessment**, or by calling the following:

800-747-4457 . . . . U.S. customers
800-465-7301 . . . . .Canadian customers
+44 (0) 113 255 5665 . . . . European customers
08 8372 0999 . . . . Australian customers
0800 222 062 . . . . .New Zealand customers
217-351-5076 . . . . .International customers

WITHDRAWN

For technical support, send an e-mail to:
support@hkusa.com . . . . U.S. and international customers
info@hkcanada.com . . . . Canadian customers
academic@hkeurope.com . . . . European customers
keycodesupport@hkaustralia.com . . . . . Australian and New Zealand customers

 HUMAN KINETICS
The Information Leader in Physical Activity & Health

11-2011

Meeting Physical Education Standards Through Meaningful Assessment

Research-Based Strategies for Secondary Teachers

Meeting Physical Education Standards Through Meaningful Assessment

Research-Based Strategies for Secondary Teachers

Greg Bert

Lisa Summers

Human Kinetics

Library of Congress Cataloging-in-Publication Data

Bert, Greg.
  Meeting physical education standards through meaningful assessment : research-based strategies for secondary teachers / Greg Bert and Lisa Summers.
      p. cm.
  Includes bibliographical references.
  1. Physical education and training--Study and teaching (Secondary) 2. Physical education and training--Curricula. 3. Physical education for children--Standards--United States. 4. Physical fitness for children--Standards--United States. I. Summers, Lisa. II. Title.
  GV365.B47 2013
  613.70712--dc23

                    2012018676

ISBN-10: 1-4504-1271-8 (print)
ISBN-13: 978-1-4504-1271-1 (print)

The web addresses cited in this text were current as of June 2012, unless otherwise noted.

Acquisitions Editor: Cheri Scott; **Developmental Editor:** Jacqueline Eaton Blakley; **Assistant Editor:** Anne Rumery; **Copyeditor:** Alisha Jeddeloh; **Permissions Manager:** Dalene Reeder; **Graphic Designer:** Nancy Rasmus; **Graphic Artist:** Denise Lowry; **Cover Designer:** Keith Blomberg; **Photographer (cover):** © Human Kinetics; **Photographer (interior):** Photos courtesy of Cherie Mortensen, Live~Laugh~Love Photography; **Art Manager:** Kelly Hendren; **Associate Art Manager:** Alan L. Wilborn; **Illustrations:** © Human Kinetics; **Printer:** United Graphics

Printed in the United States of America   10 9 8 7 6 5 4 3 2 1

The paper in this book is certified under a sustainable forestry program.

Human Kinetics
Website: www.HumanKinetics.com

United States: Human Kinetics, P.O. Box 5076, Champaign, IL 61825-5076
800-747-4457
e-mail: humank@hkusa.com

Canada: Human Kinetics, 475 Devonshire Road Unit 100, Windsor, ON N8Y 2L5
800-465-7301 (in Canada only)
e-mail: info@hkcanada.com

Europe: Human Kinetics, 107 Bradford Road, Stanningley, Leeds LS28 6AT, United Kingdom
+44 (0) 113 255 5665
e-mail: hk@hkeurope.com

Australia: Human Kinetics, 57A Price Avenue, Lower Mitcham, South Australia 5062
08 8372 0999
e-mail: info@hkaustralia.com

New Zealand: Human Kinetics, P.O. Box 80, Torrens Park, South Australia 5062
0800 222 062
e-mail: info@hknewzealand.com

E5493

To Renee, Ryan, Lindsay, and Katie. I love you all!

—Greg

To Frankie and Jake and to personal health!

—Lisa

And to the students at Black Hills High School.
May you all engage in the spirit of the game!

CONTENTS

PREFACE

How many successful people have you ever heard say, "I just make it up as I go along?" I can't think of one.

—Mike Ditka

What is a physically educated person? How do we measure this? What do we assess? This book answers all of these questions and more. It grew from a need to add validity and research to our own grading system. It also grew out of frustration after seeing students continually earning superior grades for simply showing up, dressing down, and being good students! We found it difficult to explain our grades to students and parents, and we also found that our students' grades were not accurately measuring our national, state, and district standards. We needed to change what we were assessing and how we were assessing it, and we needed to link our assessments to these standards.

We started asking ourselves what a physically educated person looks like. What are the characteristics of a physically educated person? We attended an in-service training in our school district and met a speaker who talked about what really matters—teaching students objectives, standards, and goals that will make them successful at the next level. For secondary students, this is defined as what they need to be able to do and understand in order to lead a healthy and active lifestyle. Our students need to know what is necessary in order to be active adults. We have national, state, local, and professional teaching standards to address to our students. When we add these up, we are teaching 50 to 60 components each year. We decided to simplify this process and make our grades more meaningful by identifying the standards that got our students to the next level and doing a great job teaching those standards.

This book discusses six standards that will move students into the next level of adulthood physical activity. Readers will learn how to identify a physically educated person and what to do if students are not meeting standards and are not ready to move on. This is a practical book giving teachers simple, easy-to-implement strategies to assess and evaluate students via standards-based grading.

This book is written for the secondary physical education teacher. Its purpose is to teach experienced and new teachers how to apply and use standards-based assessment (SBA) practices. This book will teach physical educators how to identify and plan quality lessons. We provide learning targets for each of our standards and ready-to-use formative and summative assessments. The assessments are based on the works and suggested teaching strategies and assessments of Rick Stiggins and Robert Marzano.

This book is significant because it gives ideas, strategies, and assessments that teachers can implement the next day, with easy-to-understand game-based drills, small-group games, and cognitive assessments. Demystifying the relationships among assessment, standards, and classroom practice, *Meeting Physical Education Standards Through Meaningful Assessment: Research-Based Strategies for Secondary Teachers* prepares teachers to create effective instruction plans. It offers teachers a framework to link standards and assessment through instruction as well as an up-to-date road map to navigate state and national education requirements.

The book is divided into three parts. Part I is the brains of the book, where you will quickly learn why you should choose SBA, you will familiarize yourself with the national standards, and you will be able to understand the importance of selecting effective strategies to improve formative and summative assessments.

The application of effective strategies in creating assessments for each standard are discussed and shared in part II of this book. We provide templates and answer keys for both formative and summative assessments.

In part III we discuss how to assess multiple standards simultaneously. In addition, we discuss how to differentiate instruction for varying abilities and needs and how to objectively assess students during activity.

This book is supplemented by a web resource that includes all of the assessments discussed throughout. Blank forms are included, as well as answer keys and samples. With these tools, you can implement your own SBA system with ease.

Teaching is part art and part science. We are dealing with real students who come with different shapes, sizes, and life experiences that can make our job both difficult and meaningful. In this book, we show you what has worked for us at Black Hills High School in the Tumwater School District and at the same time blend in educational research that supports our assessment strategies. As a NASPE STARS School, we

have been successful in identifying and producing quality physically educated students. With our National Board Certifications in physical education along with being distinguished as state, regional, and national NASPE Teachers of the Year, we hope to make your passion as a physical education teacher a bit more meaningful and easier and to help you feel more validated in your work.

We have shared our ideas with many other physical education teachers at state and district conferences. We have learned from these other professionals the need for and interest in collaborative work. Teachers want to change their current systems but struggle with how to start the process, what it can look like, and what are creative ways to improve student learning. And that's what it comes down to: This book has the building blocks to improve student learning. Teachers can get meaningful methods to assess for learning. Easy-to-read and free of technical jargon, this text focuses squarely on what teachers need to know in order to make assessment work in the classroom and gymnasium.

ACKNOWLEDGMENTS

I wish to thank my wonderful wife, Renee, who has supported me in this project and who continues to be the love of my life. My children, Ryan, Lindsay, and Katie, may you all grow and feel fulfilled in your lives the way teaching has done for me. I love you all so much! To my mom and dad, who always believed in me, and to Janice, my speech therapist, who helped me become a teacher.

I also wish to acknowledge my future, present, and former physical education students who have inspired me and taught me many lessons. To my students from Drew Junior High, Saint Stephen's School, Curtis Intermediate, San Bernardino High School, Victor Valley College, Barstow College, Barstow High School, Tumwater High School, Black Hills High School, and Saint Martin's University, I remember you, and I wish you all the best.

I wish to thank many fellow physical educators. Lisa Summers, I have had the pleasure to write and teach with you over the years at Black Hills High School. Your teaching skills and passion for our field inspire me daily. Lori Dunn, my friend and mentor, brought me into the AAHPERD, NASPE, and WAPHERD worlds! To the NASPE TOY Class of 2007: Maggie, Connie, Linda, "Tip," Kevin, Roberta, Bob, Deb, Lori, Susan, Nancy, Katie, Emily, Ulrike, Lynne, and De—your picture inspires me each day!

I had two wonderful physical education teachers when I was in junior high school: Mr. Kahn and Mr. Merriman. Thank you!

—Greg Bert

Come to the edge.
We might fall.
Come to the edge.
It's too high!
COME TO THE EDGE!
And they came
And he pushed
And they flew.

—Christopher Logue

I have had several people and experiences in my life that convinced me to take risks, pushed me into being my best self, and challenged me. Because of those people and my experiences, I enjoy a career in physical education, I enjoy a healthy and fit life, and I am passionate about life. I would like to thank the teachers, motivators, and supporters in my life.

From the day I was born, my parents have pushed me. I was told at an early age that I was valuable and important. I was encouraged through sports, activities, and academics. I was given a strong foundation of self. I knew who I was, what I wanted in life, and what I wanted to enjoy. And my parents always encouraged me to pursue those passions. Thank you, Mom and Dad, for encouraging me to come to the edge and for pushing me all these years.

My husband exemplifies support. He allows me to fly and enjoy my flight. He supports my interests and passions and partakes in all of my school commitments and extracurricular activities. Jake, I am grateful for your ongoing love and support. Thanks for reading this work and having lunches and cooked meals ready for me when I was too tired to feed myself. You make it easier for me to fly!

Without Dr. Leann Martin, who knows what type of physical education teacher I would have become? She was and still is my mentor. Her competence, with-it-ness, and professionalism truly inspired me to pursue those qualities in my own teaching. Every time she teaches, I get a new idea. She continues to improve her craft, continues to push herself creatively, and displays insightful attention to detail. Dr. Leann Martin, I applaud you, I thank you, and I am forever grateful to you for helping me to develop into a passionate and hard-working physical educator. You definitely pushed me, and I am enjoying the ride.

Greg Bert, my colleague, friend, work spouse, and coauthor, you kept pushing me to write this book with you and I am truly honored to share this experience with you. We have taught and worked side by side for many years, and it has been with great pleasure. You are entertaining, charming, witty, and a real physical educator. You remind me each day that we can make a difference in physical education, we can make an impact with our students and community, and with perseverance and hard work we can continue to vocalize the need for physical education in all schools and at all grade levels. Thanks, pal, for everything. It's been a wonderful flight with such a dear friend.

—Lisa Summers

PART I

Introduction to Standards-Based Assessment

CHAPTER 1

Getting Started With Standards-Based Assessment

Students who can identify what they are learning significantly outscore those who cannot.

—Robert J. Marzano

What does it mean to be physically educated? This key question should guide our physical education philosophy, learning objectives, outcomes, and assessment.

Standards-based assessment (SBA) is an assessment system that relies on measurable standards that describe what every student should know and be able to do. *Standards* are statements of educational goals established by district, state, and federal governing bodies. Each standard has specific and intentional *learning targets* (or *learning objectives*) that guide teaching and directly connect instruction and assessment. These learning targets are statements of what we want students to comprehend, apply, appreciate, and demonstrate. *Assessment* is the means by which we check students' progress in achieving learning targets and meeting standards. Assessment is so much more than giving a test at the end of the unit. It is an ongoing teaching process by which we continually evaluate student performance over several opportunities. If the best assessments tell us what our students are truly learning, doesn't it make sense that those assessments should be based on the standards that tell us what we want students to learn?

SBA ensures we are using academic standards as the primary focus of our instruction. The out-comes of these assessments tell us whether students are exceeding the standard, meeting it, or failing to meet it. The expectation that all students can meet a standard becomes a reality when we give students the time, feedback, and assistance that assessment requires. "The primary goal of a standards-based system is for all students to meet the standards. That is, to be competent or proficient in every aspect of the curriculum. The key is to evaluate student achievement using similar criteria, consistently applied at all levels" (O'Connor, 2007, p. 3).

Many students show up for physical education, dress down, and behave well. But why should we use these behaviors to assess learning? They are just part of what we should expect from a physical education student, and they do not indicate whether the student is physically educated. SBA gives us a way to focus our instruction on intentional educational outcomes rather than behaviors that don't necessarily reflect learning.

We have created an SBA system at Black Hills High School that identifies six power standards that coincide with the six National Association for Sport and Physical Education (NASPE) physical education standards and support the philosophy of teaching lifetime sport and fitness skills. Each power standard has a corresponding *kid-friendly objective (KFO)*, which is a simplified definition of what students should be able to learn in physical education class. We organize our philosophy, learning targets, and assessments around our power standards, each of which has its own KFO that can be easily understood by students, parents, and administrators.

What Is Standards-Based Assessment in Physical Education?

We have found that using a research-based assessment system that focuses on proficiency or mastery at a set point in time works best for our students. Our students know what we are assessing them for, and we use various teaching methodologies to get our students to mastery or proficiency.

Using SBA allows us to be objective and accurate when we grade in physical education. Because it eliminates bias, distortion, and subjectivity, students are less apt to be confused about what they are being graded on and how they are assessed. It also brings validity to how we grade our students, giving real meaning to grades and reflecting learning as students either meet or fail to meet the standards. Students receive an authentic assessment of what they understand and are able to do, which creates more student buy-in. All students have set criteria for the same work and are measured similarly, which helps ensure a grade that is accurate, timely, and fair.

Clearly communicating to our students how they are being assessed and what they are being assessed on is a vital task in SBA. Grade marks are developed and communicated to build motivation and sustained work ethic. We share with our students why they are learning and being assessed on skills, concepts, and understanding of the importance of participating in a vigorous, active, and healthy lifestyle. If we can lead our students to value what they are learning, they gain a deeper appreciation of what they are learning.

What we most appreciate about SBA is that it allows us to adapt our instruction by reflecting on students' understanding. Who met the standard? Who did not? Who exceeded it? Who didn't learn it, and who partially learned it? Answering these questions is the key to differentiating instruction within our physical education classes. We discover who needs to be challenged with deeper enrichment, who needs more instruction to meet the standard, when the class will be able to move on, what we may need to reteach, and when we may be able to provide more in-depth instruction.

Another important part of SBA is to identify and assess learning targets from standards. These learning targets ensure that we grade on academic content, which means we are not basing our grading solely on attendance, behavior, and effort. Academic content in physical education is based on movement and concepts.

We provide multiple assessment opportunities for our students to demonstrate meeting or exceeding standards. This ensures that all students, who learn at varying rates, are given opportunities to show mastery.

SBA measures what a student should know and be able to do at each grade level. This ensures both vertical and horizontal curriculum alignment. What is most apparent with SBA is evidence of learning, teacher adaptations to student needs, and alignment of teaching with standards.

What Standards-Based Assessment Is Not

The practice of teaching, testing, and moving on to the next unit, which used to be common in physical education, is not quality education. Grades determined by a bell curve, average score, or mean do not accurately measure what a student knows; they only show how students compare with each other. In addition, the older systems of assessing and grading did not give students who learn at slower rates a chance to be retaught, take retests, or demonstrate their learning to the teacher. In the past, students were rewarded for speed in learning, but we do not all learn at the same rate, and we need to accept these differences in our students.

One-time or overly weighted projects, labs, or single measures can unfairly skew grades. This high-stakes assessment is unfair, does not motivate students, and simply does not work. We need to check for understanding multiple times before we can give a project or a lab.

We also know that subjective considerations such as extra credit, attitude, dressing, neatness, showing up, and behavior do not accurately reflect our chosen standards. These are behavior or attitudinal expectations.

Using ineffective assessment practices does not help or motivate our students. Many students give up once they receive a poor grade because they do not have a chance to perform to standard. This has helped to create an "I hate physical education" attitude because there is no chance to catch up, receive help, and be assessed fairly on what they can do. We have found that if students are not successful in physical education, they choose not to take it as an elective. Students across the United States are waiving physical education, and one reason may be arbitrary grading. Once again, SBA is more effective than grading subjectively, grading by a curve, giving one test and moving on, or offering extra credit. SBA measures what a student knows and is able to do.

Steps to Create a Standards-Based Assessment System

We recommend taking the following steps to create your own SBA system.

1. **Write standards and KFOs.** For each grade level, choose your standards. These can come from state, district, and national physical education standards. The power standards we use in this book are mostly derived from the NASPE physical education standards, but they are also informed by other standards relevant to our state, district, and school. Write a corresponding KFO for each standard, and use it frequently in communicating with students, parents, and others about the standards. Chapter 2 goes into greater length about our six power standards.

2. **Organize learning targets for each standard.** Students need to know what they are expected to learn and why. Learning targets are the specific objectives for each standard that you want students to be able to demonstrate, understand, and value. They should further describe the content of each standard. You'll see detailed examples in chapter 2 of learning targets that were developed to support our six power standards.

3. **Create an assessment process.** You'll have to decide how to score assessments and how that translates to grades. We use an *E*, *M*, *PRO*, *BLS* grading system. Many may refer to our grading system as a rubric (table 1.1). It aligns with our state (Washington) assessment scoring system and allows for consistency in reporting student learning.

We use our state's performance expectations (PEs) and grade-level expectations (GLEs), the NASPE national standards for physical education, and our district's power standards as the foundation of our instructional curriculum. Therefore the report card is based on assessments of the student's learning at determined points in the year.

In a standards-based system, students are evaluated on how well they are progressing toward meeting the standards at each reporting period. Evaluation tools may include summative and performance assessments. This is the grading rubric we use to communicate level and description of student performance with concepts and skills:

TABLE 1.1 Sample Rubric

Exceeds standard (*E*)	Meets standard (*M*)	Progressing toward standard (*PRO*)	Below standard (*BLS*)
The student consistently and independently demonstrates a deeper understanding of grade-level standards and applies key knowledge, skills, and concepts beyond what is required.	The student consistently meets the grade-level standards and applies key knowledge, skills, and concepts.	The student inconsistently meets the grade-level standards. The student inconsistently applies understanding of key knowledge, skills, concepts, and processes.	The student is not meeting the standards as described and shows lack of understanding of the concepts and skills. The student is working significantly below standard in this area.
E indicates the student grasps, applies, and extends the key concepts with more complex content.	*M indicates the student met the expected level of performance. All students are working to be able to meet grade-level standards in all subjects.*	*PRO indicates the student is not able to regularly meet the established performance expectations or grade-level expectations for a given subject. Contact and planning with the home is important to bring performance up to grade level.*	*BLS indicates the student is struggling and shows serious misunderstanding of concepts and skills. Contact and planning with the home is important to bring performance up to grade level. Further diagnostic assessment might help determine the appropriate intervention and instructional support.*

3 points	=	E	=	exceeds standard	=	A
2 points	=	M	=	meets standard	=	B
1 points	=	PRO	=	progressing toward standard	=	C
0 points	=	BLS	=	below standard	=	D

Be sure to also record reteaching and retake options and policies. Note that the standard for mastery is at least 80%.

4. **Create ways to communicate assessment and grading to parents.** It's important to keep parents informed of how and why their children are being assessed and graded. There are many ways of doing this. For example, you could use a report card like the one shown in figure 1.1. This is an example of our report card that shows each summative assessment given to our students. These summative assessments are explained later in the book under each standard. You might also use a progress report, an e-mail update, a website, or an open house to stay in touch with parents. You may already have methods that work well for you, but now is a good time to consider additional or new ways to connect with parents about your plans for helping their children to become physically educated. The important thing is to make sure you clearly communicate to parents how their children are being assessed and graded.

5. **Develop and maintain a workable gradebook.** Organize grades by power standards. We recommend recording formative assessment scores but not counting them toward grades. Record summative assessment scores and count them toward grades.

Grading to Reflect Learning

Summative grades must reflect what students can show, perform, understand, and demonstrate with success. Only then will students' grades truly reflect learning!

In the brilliantly crafted book, *A Repair Kit for Grading*, author Ken O'Connor specifies 15 fixes for broken grading systems. A broken grading system is one that uses nonstandard grading criteria such as attendance, conduct, extra credit, dressing down, and other factors that do not directly measure meeting of standards. The book states that in many school districts, students are not receiving consistent, accurate, and meaningful grades that reflect student learning and that many criteria do not reflect what has been learned.

Here are some pointers for developing grading systems that reflect learning.

1. **Grades must reflect only student achievement.** Do not use desired behaviors, such as attendance, behavior, dressing, and effort, for summative grades. These desired behaviors are not a true measure of learning. However, it is a good idea to communicate students' progress in these desired behaviors in a supplemental report to parents. Rate effort by checking off persistence, striving for accuracy, time on task, and dressing. Give descriptive feedback. Give consequences for negative and off-task behaviors, such as requiring students to spend extra time after school, taking away certain privileges, and so on.

2. **Build support systems for students.** Penalties for poor performance do not accurately reflect what has been learned and actually decrease motivation to improve and to turn in missed assignments. We do not assign zeros for incomplete, missing, late, or low scores. Zeros imply that there is no hope to complete or relearn material. We allow students to turn in late or missing work, regardless of the reason, and focus on assisting students who need help with making up work. Often students do not turn in work because they do not understand the lesson. It's important to allow students to earn the grades that they need, even if this means they must make up the work late. Students all learn at varying rates.

3. **Seek specific evidence that supports higher levels of learning when giving out supplemental assignments.** Don't allow bonus points or extra credit for grades. They distort grades and do not report higher levels of learning. Any extra work opportunities should exist solely for the purpose of demonstrating higher levels of learning and should support power standards and learning goals.

4. **Organize grading information by power standard.** As you will see throughout this book, all of our assignments, assessments, and class activities relate to a power standard. To organize grading information by power standard, we first

Physical Education Report Card

Name _____   Class _____

I Am a Physically Educated Person

1. I can move correctly.

_____ Biomechanics of Human Movement Project

_____ Graphic Organizer: Yoga Bingo

_____ Graphic Organizer: Biomechanical Principle Bingo

_____ I Can Move Correctly: Self-Reflection

2. I can train myself and others.

_____ FITT Project

_____ I Can Train Myself and Others: Self-Reflection

_____ State test of health and fitness (not included)

3. I participate regularly.

_____ Physical Activity Opportunities in My Community: Parks and Recreation

_____ Physical Activity Opportunities in My Community: Fitness Industry

_____ I Participate Regularly: Self-Reflection

4. I am fit.

_____ I Am Fit Versus I Am Not Fit

_____ Fitness Tracker

_____ Fitness Log

_____ Fitness Profile

_____ I Am Fit Project

_____ I Am Fit: Self-Reflection

5. I can play fairly.

_____ Spirit of the Game Project

_____ I Can Play Fairly: Self-Reflection

6. I value physical education, fitness, and health.

_____ Sponsoring Your Own School Run

_____ SMART Fitness Goals: Cardiorespiratory Endurance

_____ SMART Fitness Goals: Muscular Endurance

_____ SMART Fitness Goals: Flexibility

_____ Self-Reflection Assignments

_____ Fitness Calendar

_____ Personal Fitness and Nutrition Log

_____ I Value Physical Education, Fitness, and Health: Self-Reflection

FIGURE 1.1 Sample report card.

identify the learning targets. Second, we design our instruction and activities based on the learning targets. Third, we select appropriate assessments that measure the learning targets.

5. **Only compare students' performance with established standards and tests.** Examples in physical education are the Fitnessgram and President's Challenge fitness tests. Do not publicly compare students' scores with national fitness norms. Also, do not base grades on group work or collaboration.

6. **Emphasize recent evidence of learning over evidence collected over time.** It does not matter when a student learned but rather that learning occurred. Early poor tests should be allowed to be retaken. Retakes and reevaluations are an ongoing process.

7. **Remember that all students are different.** Learning is developmental and students will meet standards at different points in time. Making sure students learn is what our efforts are all about.

Appropriate Practice in Physical Education

The American Alliance for Health, Physical Education, Recreation and Dance (AAHPERD) and NASPE emphasize appropriate practices to be encouraged by all physical education professions (NASPE, 2009). We support the guidelines that these organizations share with physical education professionals. They help us quickly learn effective and ineffective assessment practices and methodologies. Keep these appropriate practices in mind as you create and develop grading practices, assessments, and rubrics.

Feedback to Students

Let's take a look at effective ways to provide feedback to students. We'll also compare these effective practices with those that are ineffective.

Appropriate Practice

The teacher consistently supports the effort and successes of all students. Daily lessons are debriefed by the teacher, who provides the link between student experience and curriculum goals. Teachers provide positive, descriptive feedback for all participants, including direct descriptive feedback on student work, assignments, and skill progress. They use a variety of assessment methods so as to develop a clear

picture of student progress and achievement. The assessments include clearly defined criteria, which are articulated to students as part of instruction prior to evaluation. Grading systems reflect the degree to which students achieve the educational goals set for them. Teachers provide regular progress reports to students and parents using continual, formative evaluations. Teachers facilitate peer feedback through the use of rating scales, checklists, and task sheets. Report cards and progress reports provide regular, systematic information about student performance. Immediate updates on student progress are provided to parents through phone calls, personal notes, e-mails, or district website grading systems.

Inappropriate Practice

Students receive only general or obvious feedback. Students receive little descriptive feedback concerning performance. Teachers seldom talk to students about performance or behavior at the conclusion of the day's activity. Teacher comments may be directed to the class as a whole rather than to individuals. Feedback contains little information about the quality of the student response, how to improve, or what has been accomplished. Teachers do not inform students about the levels of achievement necessary for the various grades or how to achieve them. Reports to parents and students are infrequent, unclear, or perfunctory. Teachers assign grades based on a single skill, fitness test, or written test given at the completion of instruction. Teachers use arbitrary measures such as effort, dress, or participation that do not reflect the instructional objectives.

We encourage feedback as a key to student success. From continual feedback, students perform skills correctly, understand concepts, and gain confidence. Be specific, and provide both verbal and written feedback.

Responsible Assessment

There is a clear distinction between appropriate and inappropriate assessments in physical education. Let's take a look.

Appropriate Practice

Teachers design assessment in relation to the goals and objectives of the instructional program and planned outcomes for student achievement. Assessment is ongoing, not just at quarter-report time. Students are aware of the criteria for accomplishment of a skill, knowledge, or disposition and the rubric that will be used to assess performance.

Teachers assess student performance that demonstrates the ability to apply, analyze, synthesize, and evaluate various concepts related to motor skills, fitness, and physical activity participation. Fitness testing is a source of feedback used to improve personal health-related fitness and to progress toward personal goals. Teachers conduct skill and fitness assessments discreetly and with a conscious effort to avoid putting students in the spotlight. Responsible assessment is also a way to communicate program successes to the community.

Inappropriate Practice

Students are not assessed regularly or are assessed on isolated measurements. Students are assessed using inconsistent, arbitrary measures that do not reflect the instructional objectives or learning opportunities. Often assessment is limited to attendance, dressing for activity, compliance with class rules, and subjective observation. Teachers use rubrics and criteria but do not share them with students, so the students do not know what they need to be able to do. Fitness testing determines grades. Teachers do not respect student confidentiality when conducting assessments; students perform skills for a grade as the rest of the class sits nearby and watches.

The goal of this book is to help teachers be prepared with research-based, planned, and intentional assessments that measure skills, concepts, and values based on the national standards for physical education. We guide you with a variety of effective strategies for helping your students to meet your established standards. Our role as physical educators is more than just teaching and testing; we need to check along the way to see if students are meeting the desired learning targets.

Variety of Assessments

Let's quickly review how we can use a variety of assessments in our classes. We will also describe inappropriate practices in this area.

Appropriate Practice

Teachers systematically teach and assess all domains (cognitive, affective, and physical). Teachers use a variety of assessment methods, such as portfolios, journals, multimedia presentations, Internet research, charts, and graphs, to view student performance in many ways and to get a broad picture of student learning. Teachers plan assessments that reflect student learning about physical activity as well as performance. Teachers evaluate student participation in

outside-of-class activities. Formative assessment is done frequently and regularly as part of learning. Numerous indicators are considered in summative assessments of student achievement.

Assessments need to showcase comprehension of the targeted skills, concepts, and values and the ability to apply them. Physical education is the rare subject that assesses movement, physical ability, and readiness. A one-size-fits-all approach to all activities, concepts, and students is the wrong approach. We need to provide multiple approaches and multiple opportunities for students to demonstrate that they can meet our learning targets and standards.

Inappropriate Practice

Teachers use assessment infrequently, and summative assessment is based on a single performance or incident. Teachers do not use a variety of measures because creating these measures and evaluating the performance results would take too much time.

Fitness Testing

Being able to distinguish how we can access fitness without subjectivity, and the training to be able to be successful. Accessing fitness requires teachers to compare their students to national norms. Teachers do this by reporting scores and sharing them individually with their students. Assigning a letter grade to a fitness score is contraindicated because of genetic and developmental reasons. Teaching students how to train so that they may be able to train themselves is very important.

Appropriate Practice

Teachers use fitness assessment as part of the ongoing process of helping students understand, enjoy, improve, and maintain their physical fitness and well-being (e.g., students set goals for improvement that are revisited during the school year). As part of an ongoing physical education program, students are prepared physically in each fitness component so that they can complete the assessments safely (e.g., students train appropriately before running a mile) (AAHPERD, 2009, p. 22).

Inappropriate Practice

Teachers use fitness tests to assign grades. Students are required to run a mile (1.6 km) without appropriate conditioning or acclimatization or are expected to perform pull-ups without prior conditioning or strength training.

We do not grade our students on physical fitness testing. For the reasons stated thus far and in the following list, grading fitness tests can turn students away from physical education and physical activity. Physical fitness testing has been a common thread in U.S. physical education programs since the late 1950s. The approach since then has been to fight obesity by measuring and grading physical fitness scores, but obesity continues to rise and is currently one of our greatest health care expenditures. The mainstream approach of grading fitness scores is not working and actually hurts our profession. In addition, physical fitness testing does not take into account the physical benefits of medium- and low-intensity activities.

There are many reasons to not grade physical fitness scores:

- Some students have a genetic predisposition toward physical fitness (Bouchard et al, 1999; Pangrazi & Corbin, 1990).
- Nutrition, climate, and air pollution can affect performance (Pangrazi & Darst, 2006).
- Trainability can be genetic (Bouchard et al., 1992).
- Students grow and mature at different rates (Pangrazi & Darst, 2006).
- Some students perform better at tests than others (Pangrazi & Darst, 2006).
- Time allotments in physical education class are limited and prevent full training.
- Many boys physically mature into their early 20s, well after high school.
- Students who score well in fitness testing are not necessarily the most active (Pangrazi & Darst, 2006).
- Most fitness improvements in elementary school students are due to normal growth and development (Pangrazi, 2007).
- Some students do not respond well to training (Bouchard, 1993a).
- Preadolescent youth show little physiological response to training (Payne & Morrow, 1993).
- Scoring fitness results creates an unfortunate hierarchy of good versus poor and healthy versus unhealthy among young people.
- Fitness testing does not take into account the benefits of moderate-intensity exercise (Pangrazi, 2007).

Grading

We must ensure that our grading practices and policies are sound and fair to all of our students. The following guidelines will assist in this process.

Appropriate Practice

Grades are based on thoughtfully identified criteria that align with course goals and national standards. Students know the criteria included in their grades and the rationale behind them.

Inappropriate Practice

Grades are based on athletic ability, a one-time fitness or skill test, dressing requirements and attendance, or undefined measures of effort, participation, and attitude. Teachers use subjective measures (e.g., effort, participation, attitude) to assign grades.

Reprinted from *Appropriate Instructional Practice Guidelines for Elementary, Middle School and High School Physical Education* with permission from National Association for Sport and Physical Education (NASPE), 1900 Association Drive, Reston, VA 20191, www.NASPEinfo.org.

Grading Motor Skills

We assess motor skills, but we do not grade them. We believe that grading students' motor skills is poor practice. Historically, physical education teachers have tested motor skills in order to evaluate students, but this might be one of the reasons why generations of adults reflect disapprovingly upon their physical education experiences. We also do not grade students for improvement, as we will explain later (Schmidt, 1991). Teachers can begin to reverse this trend by focusing more on the unskilled and unfit students. This raises the question, do we need to produce highly skilled students? No. Can students be physically active and unskilled in sport? Yes.

Developing skills is important, but it should not be factored into grading and evaluation, which assess learning. True learning is a change in habit strength, which is permanent change in performance (Schmidt, 1991). Assessing motor skills to point out strengths and areas where students can improve is appropriate. We assess motor skills to help students understand strategies for improvement. The problem with skills testing for grading purposes is that many differences in students' skills can be attributed to differences in normal growth and development, factors that are beyond anyone's control (Haywood & Getchell, 2001).

Another reason not to grade on skill development is that skill success depends on specific practice (the training principle of specificity), and students do not have equal access to practice opportunities. Students who put time into sport and games tend to be more successful than students who do not. We simply do not have the time in physical education classes to spend the hours and hours it takes to develop highly skilled athletes, and this is not our direction anyway! For example, we have all noticed that the students who put in hours of tennis practice tend to be better tennis players at the high school and recreational levels. Some students have vastly greater skills, experience, and teaching and coaching due to being on club teams. These students have advantages over students who have not had such experiences and opportunities.

Students can be both active and unskilled in sport at the same time. We have found that many students do not like competitive games or sport. This type of student would rather lift weights, run the track, hike, cycle, and perform other individual fitness activities. The term *unskilled* is relative. A student may not be skilled in tennis but highly skilled in long-distance running. Who is to say which skill is most important?

Here are some reasons to not grade for performance or improvement:

- Individual differences in growth, development, and genetics influence performance of motor skills (Haywood & Getchess, 2001; Pangrazi & Darst, 2006).

- Motor performance in males is related to skeletal maturity. Physically mature students perform better in motor tasks due to stronger, healthier, more developmentally mature bone and neuromuscular development, thus creating an unfair advantage on motor skill grading (Pangrazi & Darst, 2006).

- It is difficult to find true skills tests that are valid, reliable, objective, and peer reviewed (Pangrazi, 2007; Schmidt, 1975).

- Novelty and past experience with skill influence success. The more familiar the skill and the greater the past experience with it, the greater the success. When new and novel skills are taught, students have a lower success rate until experience and repetition with the skill produce motor skill proficiency (Schmidt, 1975).

- True learning is measured as change in habit strength, not temporary change in performance (Schmidt, 1975).

- True change in learning can be only evaluated when all learners begin at the same level, which is hard to facilitate and objectify (Schmidt, 1991).

- Motivation and fatigue affect learning (Schmidt, 1975).

- Grading for skill improvement is not justified because the law of diminishing returns affects skill performance. Highly skilled students may show less improvement than new learners.

- Testing and grading unskilled students may discourage active participation in the future.

- Typical physical education classes do not give adequate time for students to master the skills that are often graded.

- Learners usually select activities that they can be successful in (Pangrazi & Darst, 2006). Some learners will not be motivated to improve their skills, choosing to play with the skill they possess.

- Grading for skill rewards the more skilled students (Pangrazi & Darst, 2006).

- Grading for improvement rewards the more unskilled students (Schmidt, 1975).

- Skills testing takes up a lot of learning time (Pangrazi & Darst, 2006).

- Students with greater size and strength have an advantage (Pangrazi & Darst, 2006).

The Big Picture

Following are the four questions that guide our instruction as we use effective strategies and practices to improve student learning.

1. **What do we want students to know and be able to do?**

These come from our power standards and learning targets.

2. **How will we know that they've learned it?**

We use standard-based assessments, checking for understanding and analyzing results.

3. **What will we do if they haven't learned it?**

We will address this by establishing an intervention, reteaching, and using differentiated instruction practices (see chapter 12 for more on differentiated instruction).

4. **What will we do if they already know it?**

We can challenge our students by using differentiated instruction. What we have learned from research and from assessing our students is that the more we assess, the more our students know and understand.

We hope that you have a better understanding of what an SBA system looks like and what it includes. We shared what SBA is and what it is not and looked at NASPE's and our position on assessment and grading practices. In the next chapter, we share our six power standards that are based on the six NASPE standards—what we feel all of our students should be able to demonstrate, appreciate, and understand in their development as physically educated people.

CHAPTER 2

Power Standards

Develop a passion for learning. If you do, you will never cease to grow.

—Anthony J. D'Angelo

At Black Hills High School, we have aligned our instruction with the six NASPE standards that represent a physically educated person, along with various state and district standards. We call them our *power standards*, and they represent what a student needs to be able to demonstrate, apply, understand, value, and respect in order to be successful and reach the next grade level. They are absolutely necessary to teach in order to ensure the success of our students. The research also supports the fact that state test scores rise when teachers teach toward content standards (Doherty, 2003). Each power standard includes learning targets and assessments designed to measure whether students are achieving the standard. Our power standards and their associated learning targets are clear and measurable, and they represent our definition of a physically educated student.

We have also restated our six power standards into kid-friendly objectives (KFOs). For example, "I can move correctly" is the KFO for power standard 1, which covers motor skill competencies. These KFOs help our students, parents, and community understand what we are asking students to demonstrate, apply, comprehend, value, and respect.

We write the power standards and learning targets on the whiteboard each day so students know which ones we are directing our instruction toward. Because of this, we rarely get questions such as, "Why are we learning how to hit a tennis ball today?" Our power standards are known to our students. They are what we assess, and they are advertised on posters in our gyms and fitness spaces, highlighted on written assessments, and showcased in their grades at the end of the term. Students read these power standards and understand the requirements and expectations of our class, district, and state. We have listed which national standard each power standard aligns with, and we have defined each of the power standards, too—in short, this chapter explains what it looks like to be a physically educated person in our school and district.

The learning targets associated with each power standard allow teachers to focus instruction to specific content that has been identified, taught, and assessed according to the standard. *Learning targets* are the specific content, behaviors, and objectives that make up a power standard. They are measurable and detailed descriptions of what students should be able to perform, understand, and value. For example, for power standard 1 (KFO: "I can move correctly"), one of the learning targets is for students to be able to perform, understand, and apply the five biomechanical principles of human movement: opposition, weight transfer, torque, tracking, and follow-through. This learning target organizes our instruction around teaching and assessing these five biomechanical principles. Learning targets give teachers the freedom to teach and reteach toward mastery. They also provide a classroom culture where instruction is valued and expected. Our book provides the layers of assessments that characterize a classroom where learning targets are the focus. Lessons are paced according to mastery of the learning targets.

In this chapter, we define each power standard, point out pertinent research, and explain and label our learning targets. Table 2.1 outlines the six power standards and NASPE standards with the corresponding KFOs.

Power Standard 1

Student demonstrates competency in motor skills and movement patterns needed to perform a variety of physical activities.

KFO: I can move correctly.

The intent of this standard is to introduce, develop, and refine several skills. Proficiency in locomotor skills, nonlocomotor skills, combined skills, complex skills, and specialized skills will establish a strong foundation of movement. When students are proficient in or have mastered skills, they are more likely to do well in lifetime activities, fitness, sport, and games. The focus of skill

attainment looks quite different in elementary, middle, and high school, progressing from basic (e.g., skipping, running, catching, throwing) to more advanced (e.g., overhead smash in badminton, 64-count dance routine).

Our job is not to make highly skilled athletes; it is to provide students with a basic skill set that will enable them to experience some success in physical activity. All students can experience some success regarding their motor skills, but some are more successful than others due to individual differences (Schmidt, 1975, 1991). The more students use specific sport and lifetime fitness skills, the more experience and success they will encounter. This leads to enjoyment of the activity, followed by a greater likelihood that students will want to come back to the particular activity—resulting in a more physically active and skilled person. In addition, teaching skills allows students to experience success by keeping the ball in play, maintaining possession, pointing out common errors to themselves and others, and understanding how skills transfer to various sports. This should be the focus of skills teach-

TABLE 2.1 Comparison of Power Standards, NASPE Standards, and Kid-Friendly Objectives

Power standard	NASPE standard	Kid-friendly objective (KFO)
Standard 1. Student demonstrates competency in motor skills and movement patterns needed to perform a variety of physical activities.	**National standard 1.** Demonstrates competency in motor skills and movement patterns needed to perform a variety of physical activities.	I can move correctly.
Standard 2. Student is able to create and implement a fitness plan according to body-type needs, goals, and fitness maintenance.	**National standard 2.** Demonstrates understanding of movement concepts, principles, strategies, and tactics as they apply to the learning and performance of physical activities.	I can train myself and others.
Standard 3. Student applies the FITT principle weekly. Student seeks activity and regularly participates in sport, games, and fitness.	**National standard 3.** Participates regularly in physical activity.	I participate regularly.
Standard 4. Student acquires the knowledge of skills necessary to maintain a health-enhancing level of physical fitness.	**National standard 4.** Achieves and maintains a health-enhancing level of physical fitness.	I am fit.
Standard 5. Student exhibits responsible personal and social behavior that respects self and others in physical activity settings.	**National standard 5.** Exhibits responsible personal and social behavior that respects self and others in physical activity settings.	I can play fairly.
Standard 6. Student chooses to live a healthy and fit life.	**National standard 6.** Values physical activity for health, enjoyment, challenge, self-expression, and social interaction.	I value physical education, fitness, and health.

ing. We want to ignite the spark that will make students want to learn more and play outside of the school day and hopefully into adulthood. There are many adult opportunities to engage in lifetime sport.

When assessing motor skills, there are many variables regarding skill levels that teachers cannot control: natural growth and development, environmental factors, culture and background, past experiences with sport and games, age of the students, and so on (Gladwell, 2008). Because of these limiting factors, we often assess student skills in a closed environment; that is, the students demonstrate the five biomechanical principles to us or to each other. For instance, students could swing a tennis racket using the forehand groundstroke without actually hitting a ball, demonstrating opposition, weight transfer, torque, follow-through, and tracking. Students thus can be assessed in a safe and predictable environment (Schmidt, 1991).

There are many good reasons to assess motor skills:

- Changes in performance take place over time with practice (Schmidt, 1975).

- Practice plays a major role in the success and learning of new skills (Baddeley, 1998).

- Assessing and providing quality feedback results in better retention of motor skills (Singer, 1957).

- Long-term retention of motor skills depends upon regular practice (Singer, 1957).

- Evidence suggests that learning is never finished (Crossman, 1959; Schmidt, 1975).

- Performance improves with feedback, or knowledge of results (Schmidt, 1975).

- Neuroplasticity may explain positive changes in task performance (Jensen, 2006).

- Motor learning induces functional and anatomical changes in the neural circuits in the brain (Doyon & Benali, 2005).

- Aerobic activity is associated with increased learning comprehension (Ratey, 2008).

- The skilled and unskilled can improve performance. Skilled learners will show less improvement (Schmidt, 1978).

- Assessing to improve, inform, and provide feedback is important to the learning process (Heritage & Chen, 2005).

- Assessing demonstrates to students where they stand, highlights their strengths and weaknesses, and allows teachers to check for understanding and plan future lessons (Fisher & Frey, 2007).

Learning Targets

Our first learning target for standard 1 is that students can identify and apply five biomechanical principles of human movement: opposition, weight transfer, torque, tracking, and follow-through. We teach a wide variety of team, individual, and dual sports as part of our curriculum. We have chosen these five biomechanical principles that are common to all of the sports that we teach so that students can easily apply them to other sports. We have a variety of assessments that measure when students can understand, demonstrate, and apply each of the principles, which they should achieve by the end of the school year. Ultimately they will be able to teach themselves when they are away from a school setting and are introduced to new sports.

The five biomechanical principles that we include in our rubric and teach our students for each skill are as follows (Haywood & Getchell, 2001):

- Opposition—facing sideways or perpendicular to the target

- Weight transfer and stepping power—for example, weight shifting from back foot to front foot, as in the baseball swing

- Torque—twisting power, as when the hips and shoulders begin facing perpendicular to a target and twist to facing the target, such as in the baseball swing

- Tracking—keeping the eyes on the ball or pointing to the target

- Follow-through—the ending phase of a movement to the opposite side of the body, as when the forehand tennis groundstroke swing for a right-handed player is initiated on the right side of the body and finishes on the left side of the body over the left shoulder

Although we have identified other biomechanics (Hay, 1985), such as force application, balance, and others, we believe in simplifying biomechanics for students. For example, force application can also be implied via weight transfer and torque. Balance can be taught via weight transfer.

These biomechanics can be assessed through teacher observation, student self-analysis, and peer observation. The five biomechanics can be used in many sports and activities and are therefore attractive to us as teachers (Schmidt, 1991). In addition, our students have come to understand what each biomechanical principle means in our lifetime sport curriculum.

The second learning target for standard 1 is that students are able to discuss, evaluate, and assess common strategies in sport and games. Many team and individual sports share common strategies. By teaching common strategies, teachers can quickly get their students active because they are familiar with basic offensive and defensive strategies. We divide our common strategies into two groups: sport and games, and racket sports.

For sport and games, strategies include the following:

- Moving to open space
- Coming to the ball
- Guarding your person
- Being hard to guard
- Using specific communication
- Facing the ball to receive
- Using width and depth (players in front, side, or behind ball or object)
- Person-to-person defending

For racket sports and games, our strategies focus on five ways to control a ball or like object via striking, kicking, or throwing:

- Height
- Distance and depth
- Direction
- Spin (rotation of the ball)
- Pace (speed of the ball)

Students can use these ball-control methods as an offensive threat.

Power Standard 2

Student is able to create and implement a fitness plan according to body-type needs, goals, and fitness maintenance.

KFO: I can train myself and others.

This standard concerns the ability to use cognitive information to understand and enhance motor skill acquisition, performance, and fitness. We want students to understand all aspects of an appropriate, safe, and intentional workout plan and lifestyle. We call these our *cognitive concepts*, and they also are included in the learning targets of this standard:

- Benefits of exercise—These include increased life span, decreased risk of cardiovascular disease, increased physical fitness and health, lower resting pulse rate and blood pressure, and lower blood lipid levels (CDC, 2011).

- Five physical fitness components—These are cardiorespiratory endurance, muscular endurance, muscular strength, flexibility, and body composition.

- FITT principle—Stands for **f**requency (how often one trains), **i**ntensity (how hard one trains), **t**ime (how long one trains), and **t**ype of activity. Students also learn how the principle relates to each fitness component.

- SPORT training principles—These include **s**pecificity (training for the specific type of activity), **p**rogression (gradually increasing the workload of the exercise), **o**verload (the amount of work performed), **r**eversibility (losing the training effects when one does not train), and **t**edium (adding variety to the workout in order to progress). To help explain these principles, we will use a person wanting to improve her mile time as an example.
  - Specificity—It is necessary to run in order to improve as a runner.
  - Progression—Increase frequency of running, increase overload training, and change intensity.
  - Overload—Increase the workload through distance, intensity, change in terrain, grade (incline), speed, hill training, and so on.
  - Reversibility—Stopping can inhibit the ability to make gains or sustain abilities.
  - Tedium—Doing the same workout or training will not improve performance.

When students understand and learn how to apply these cognitive concepts, they will be more likely to apply them through their adult years. They will be able to train themselves and others when they leave the school setting and enter the adult world. If we were to look at the common thread between all of our physical education classes, we would find that these cognitive concepts are the common denominator within our curriculum.

It's important to facilitate the development and maintenance of physical fitness. Our instruction emphasizes the techniques of training for fitness, setting personal goals, and adjusting programs for age, injury, or disability. It is critical that we convey to our students the fact that physical fitness is not just a high school experience but provides a lifetime of benefits that can be maintained by well-planned and well-executed participation in physical activity.

Power standard 2 is highly cognitive. There are times in physical education when students need to show mastery of these concepts on paper. We try to make these times short and not use long lectures. We attempt to teach as many of the learning targets in a movement setting as possible. For example, after a brief explanation of muscle endurance, we have students perform push-ups to exhaustion to teach and demonstrate muscle endurance.

Learning Targets

- **Students understand, apply, and appreciate the components of physical fitness: cardiorespiratory endurance, muscular endurance, muscular strength, flexibility, and body composition.** We identify the five fitness components as learning targets because they are research based and scientifically accepted as the definition of being physically fit. Students need to understand the five fitness components in order to plan their own exercise program and stay healthy for a lifetime; thus, these components represent foundational knowledge for all physical training. The fitness components help determine what to train when it comes to formulating an exercise plan. For example, if a student desires to improve his strength, he will train for muscular strength.

- **Students know and value the physical, mental, and social benefits of vigorous exercise and physical activity.** We want students to understand and be able to apply as many health benefits as possible to acquire the positive effects on the body, mind, and emotions. When students under-

stand why it is important to exercise, they are more apt to engage in physical activity.

- **Students show mastery of the FITT and SPORT training principles to design physical activity and sport training programs.** When teaching students how to exercise effectively, we teach nine training principles that can be taught using two kid-friendly acronyms, *FITT* and *SPORT*. These represent how to train for each fitness component or a specific sport. When students understand how the principles work together, they can then plan and follow an exercise program. Following an exercise program will help keep students at a normal weight with normal blood lipid levels, which is beneficial for optimal health. The FITT principle is a guide for improving and maintaining normal levels of the fitness components. For example, when teaching students how to train and improve their cardiorespiratory endurance, the teacher can begin by telling students how often to train the heart and lungs (frequency). The SPORT training principles are a framework for training in a specific sport, game, or fitness component. This can be seen when the teacher who is discussing training for cardiorespiratory endurance points out to students not only how often they should train the heart and lungs but also what specific activities (specificity) can improve cardiorespiratory endurance. FITT and SPORT work together when it comes to training for physical fitness.

Power Standard 3

Student applies the FITT principle weekly. Student seeks activity and regularly participates in sport, games, and fitness.

KFO: I participate regularly.

The intent of this standard is to help students establish patterns of regular participation in meaningful physical activity (60 minutes of physical activity each day). This standard should connect what is done in the physical education class with students' lives outside of class. Participation within the physical education class is important, but what the student does outside of class is critical to developing an active, healthy lifestyle. Students are more likely to participate if they have had opportunities to develop interests that are personally meaningful. Attainment of this standard develops an awareness of those opportunities and encourages a broad level of participation. It also increases students' understanding of the relationship between physical activity and health.

Active students tend to become active adults (Talama, 2005). We need to make sure that students enjoy physical activity and look forward to its benefits. Remembering that all students can be physically active is important. Being physically active may look different from person to person, but physical activity is for everyone. Some students will prefer lifetime fitness activities or lifetime sport. Some may prefer moderate-intensity or more vigorous activities. There are benefits to both, and students need to understand that both are important.

We look at physical activity as the common denominator in physical education. Not every student will come to us physically fit or highly skilled, but most will have the ability to be physically active. Humans are wired for being active; our ancestors depended upon being active for their survival—survival of the fittest, indeed (Forencich, 2006). Physical activity and physical education help the students who need them most—the unskilled and the unfit.

Focus on the long-term benefits of activity, but teach students how to write short-term goals. We suggest SMART goals—short-term goals should be **s**pecific to the needs of the individual, **me**asurable, **a**chievable, **r**ealistic, and **t**imely. For example, here is a SMART goal:

Specific: I want to run an 8-minute mile.
Measurable: Timed with a stopwatch.
Achievable: I am healthy and able to participate in running.
Realistic: My current mile time is 8:33.
Timely: I have an entire year to get my time from 8:35 to 8:00.

There are many ways to measure physical activity, such as keeping track of time; self-reporting activities; keeping logs, diaries, or journals; making observations; monitoring heart rate; and using pedometers (Morgan, Pangrazi, & Beighle, A., 2003). It is simple to assign physical activity assignments because most can be performed during the students' leisure time and at their own pace. It is also wise to have students measure physical activity in class so that they will know how to measure activity outside of class,

especially when using pedometers and heart rate monitors. If available and appropriate, teaching young people how to use treadmills, spin bikes, elliptical trainers, exercise balls, yoga mats, free weights, and machine weights will help prepare students for outside-of-school group and individual fitness experiences.

Homework assignments that ask students to assess physical activity are a good method to extend the learning of the school day as well as promote lifelong physical activity. Remember, students accumulate most of their activity outside of school! Students will need to be very familiar with the content to do homework, but homework provides more practice in being physically active, reinforces the importance of physical activity, and prepares students for a lifetime of activity. Homework also prepares students for new content and elaborates on content discussed in class (Marzano, 2001). When students turn in logs, diaries, journals, and other assignments, learning can be further increased when the teacher writes comments on the assignments (Walberg, 1999). Research has reported that writing comments on homework has a positive effect (Marzano, 2001). Finally, homework needs to be used to extend the learning, never as extra credit or makeup work. Extra credit and makeup work do not reflect what the student knows and are not part of standards-based grading (O'Connor, 2007).

We need to teach students that physical activity is a lifestyle and a long-term commitment. We must teach them how to be active by instructing them in the skills needed for both lifetime fitness and lifetime sport activities. Because physical activity is a personal matter, some students will engage in lifetime sport activities such as tennis, golf, squash, volleyball, and basketball leagues, and some will engage in lifetime fitness opportunities such as running, cycling, and swimming. We must also teach students where to go to be active and how to locate opportunities for physical activity, such as local park and recreation departments, fitness clubs, city leagues, running trails, and safe roads for cycling.

The Centers for Disease Control and Prevention (CDC) and AAHPERD, both recommend 60 minutes of physical activity each day (CDC, 2012; AAHPERD, 2008). Physical education does not provide 60 minutes of daily physical activity due to time constraints and other nonactive class situations. (NASPE recommends that 50% of the time in physical education be spent in physical activity.) This by no means excuses students from getting 60 minutes of physical activity each day; they need to fulfill the bulk of their activity demands outside of the classroom. Because there is not enough time in class to spend 60 minutes in physical activity, it is important to teach students about physical activity opportunities offered after school and in the community.

To summarize, the most important part of physical education is teaching students how to be active outside of school. Remember, most of our students' time spent in physical activity will not be with us but out in the community. We must stress both lifetime fitness and lifetime sport opportunities. In secondary education, often students will have just one or two years of high school physical education. Our physical education class could be the last one they take. We need to make the time count by teaching students how to be physically active.

Learning Targets

Most of students' physical activity takes place outside of a class setting. Therefore, the purpose of standard 3 and its learning targets is to teach students where to find opportunities to extend their physical activity in order to live a healthy and productive lifestyle. Here are the learning targets for this standard:

- **Students can locate and access opportunities for physical activity within the school setting.** There are many opportunities for physical activity within the school setting. We introduce students to intramural activities, athletic competition, after-school clubs, after-school tournaments, and running events.
- **Students can locate and access opportunities for physical activity within the community.** Many of our assessments measure the ability to find opportunities in the community. We teach our students how to sign up for runs and other fitness events; find and research fitness clubs, local park and recreation lifetime sport activities, community club sports, sport leagues, and local fitness events; and log their experiences such as steps, miles, and minutes for any type of physical activity.
- **Students understand the similarities and differences between physical edu-**

cation and physical activity. We teach students to compare and contrast physical activity and physical education, because it is important for students to understand that physical education is a school experience that will prepare them for a lifetime of physical activity outside of the school setting. We want students to understand the value of physical education as the spark that ignites their fire for a lifetime journey in physical activity. We want students to become adults who understand the importance of physical education and support physical education programs in the future.

- **Students can demonstrate participation in physical activity within the standards set by the CDC.** The CDC is a valuable resource for information pertaining to varying forms of physical activity and their health benefits. We teach students the importance of this resource and how to use it by giving assignments that require researching information from the CDC.
- **Students understand the differences between lifetime fitness activities and lifetime sport activities.** To help students live an active lifestyle, we teach them noncontact sports that they can play for a lifetime, such as racket sports, golf, and others. We believe lifetime sports are the activities that students will continue to participate in as adults. We also recognize that not everyone cares to play a sport, so we teach students how to train themselves and find lifetime fitness activities that pertain to the five fitness components, such as running, swimming, cycling, and walking events.
- **Students understand the three types of physical activity: aerobic, muscle strengthening, and bone strengthening (CDC, 2008).** The CDC has information pertaining to low-intensity, moderate-intensity, and high-intensity physical exercise that will challenge people in the low, medium, and high target heart rate ranges. This is important because not everyone is able to participate at the high levels of their target heart rate zones. We also show students information from the CDC about such activities.

Power Standard 4

Student acquires the knowledge of skills necessary to maintain a health-enhancing level of physical fitness.

KFO: I am fit.

The intent of this standard is to help each student achieve a health-enhancing level of physical fitness. We need to encourage our students to meet or exceed suggested healthy scores on fitness tests that measure the five fitness components. Health-related fitness components include cardiorespiratory endurance, muscular strength, muscular endurance, flexibility, and body composition.

In order to meet standard 4, our main concern is increasing physical activity. Teachers and physical education departments must focus on lifelong learning and long-term lifestyle changes where physical activity is a way of life. There are many reasons why we should assess (but not grade!) physical fitness scores. We need to teach students the differences between fitness assessment and fitness grading and the reasons why we do not grade for fitness. There are many limitations to grading fitness scores, including genetic, environmental, and nutritional factors (Pangrazi & Darst, 2006). We do assess students' physical fitness scores as they relate to the healthy fitness zones set up by the Cooper Institute. Each fitness component has a range of healthy fitness scores compared with peers nationwide based on age and sex. Although this is a limited snapshot of personal fitness, it lets students know where they stand in relation to their peers. Physical fitness testing also motivates some students and indicates that training is taking effect. In addition, SMART goals can be established according to these test results.

Although we do not grade physical fitness scores, we do assess physical fitness and use the scores to teach students how to set goals, strive for healthy scores, mark and emphasize improvement, and self-test so that fitness testing can be private and geared to the individual. Physical fitness testing is appropriate when we do not put a value on the scores. Keep the scores private and use the testing exercises to give students examples of movements to engage in activity and training that target fitness components. For example, the mile run for time, the 20-meter PACER run, and the 12-minute run or walk tests are excellent examples of exercises for cardiorespiratory endurance training. By engaging in these activities, students will understand that they are excellent activities to perform three to four days a

week for the cardio portion of their exercise plans. Performing sit-ups for 1 minute or as many as possible to exhaustion will teach students how to improve endurance in their abdominal muscles.

Practice by doing leads to 75% greater retention rates compared with a lecture, written article, audiovisual presentation, or teacher demonstration. Students who learn how to train each other (their classmates) in each physical fitness component will further improve retention of fitness knowledge. We learn at a 90% retention rate when we teach the content to others (National Training Laboratories, 1997).

Student assessment of their fitness scores according to national fitness standards is best done in private. Teachers who verbally record scores or post scores on a bulletin board can cause needless embarrassment and loss of self-esteem. Fitness testing should only serve as a look at how students compare with their peers in regard to fitness tests and as a starting point for setting personal fitness goals toward becoming physically fit. Rarely should we discuss fatness with students; students need to focus on fitness rather than fatness. When the focus is upon fitness, other deficits will improve.

One way to keep fitness personal is to give students the tools for locating fitness evaluations, such as online fitness calculators. (Any search on the Internet will result in a plethora of fitness calculators.) Daily step counts can also be calculated into mileage. With this information obtained from either fitness testing or step equivalents from physical education class, students are able to answer teacher-directed questions on homework for self-reflection and extended learning opportunities. These assignments allow students to reflect on their fitness levels and set goals for improvement or maintenance. This creates accountability regarding fitness scores without putting a value on the score or putting too much emphasis (i.e., grades) on physical fitness scores.

Assessments of current fitness include all five components of fitness (cardiorespiratory endurance, muscular strength, muscular endurance, flexibility, and body composition). These fitness levels are compared with minimum health-related standards that have been developed for children of the same age and gender.

The basic measurements consist of three phases: baseline, goal setting, and posttraining. Phase 1 consists of the baseline measurements. Its purpose is to gather information about the students' beginning fitness levels. Each item is designed to measure one of the five components of fitness. By finding a starting point, students develop an awareness of where they are on the fitness and health continuum. It is important that students do not view this as a competition but rather as a starting point to improve personal fitness.

The goal-setting phase is essential to the program and is done as soon as phase 1 is complete. During this phase, students set realistic goals for each of the fitness measurements. After the goals are set, students begin to work toward improvement using a curriculum that is designed to help them reach their goals.

The culminating phase of this unit consists of post-training measurements. The data provide students with proof of how a focused approach improves fitness. All students have the opportunity to take pride in achieving their personal goals. This systematic approach to the development of fitness begins to place value on maintaining or improving individual fitness levels. The process builds excitement in students as they discover they have the power to improve their fitness and health. This is also an ideal time to match fitness goals according to the five SPORT training principles: specificity, progression, overload, reversibility, and tedium. At the end of the course, posttraining measurements are conducted to access goals.

We use the following physical fitness tests as formative assessments. The tests tell students where they stand with their peers on a national level and help them set their own goals. These standardized tests come from Fitnessgram and Focused Fitness Co. They enable students to understand and analyze personal strengths and weaknesses and give students opportunities to apply the training principles to maintain or improve scores to healthy fitness zones. We use these physical fitness assessments because they are research-based, standardized fitness measurements that are both reliable and valid. In addition, students can compare themselves with their peers nationwide. Here are the fitness assessments that we use for each fitness component.

Cardiorespiratory Endurance Assessments

- Cooper 12-minute run or walk
- Mile run
- 20-meter or 15-meter PACER run
- Rockport walking test
- Timed continuous run (12 minutes, 15 minutes, 20 minutes, 30 minutes)

Muscular Endurance

- PACER crunch test
- Sit-ups to exhaustion
- Flexed arm hang or pull-ups

Muscular Strength

- Push-ups to exhaustion
- PACER push-ups

Flexibility

- Sit-and-reach
- Trunk flexion
- Shoulder stretch

Body Composition

Body-fat percentage (skin calipers)—Although this is a good measure for body fat, it is not recommended in the school setting; this is why we do not put a lot of emphasis on body composition.

Learning Targets

- **Students can achieve targeted levels of fitness as measured through fitness testing and assessments (e.g., Fitnessgram, President's Challenge, state, district, and school fitness testing).** We present the healthy fitness zones (HFZ) from the Cooper Institute's Fitnessgram battery of physical fitness tests in each of the five fitness components. We use this battery and the corresponding zones because they are based on research and are widely accepted as the standard of physical fitness testing. Healthy fitness zones offer students the ability to self-test and learn if they are in healthy or unhealthy zones. We want students to learn about their scores so that they can adjust their training regimens.

- **Students understand and analyze personal areas of strengths and weaknesses and apply training principles to maintain or improve scores to healthy fitness zones.** This learning target is designed to give students a reference point as to where they stand in regard to healthy fitness zones for each fitness component. By doing this, students can modify their fitness plans to improve or maintain their personal fitness programs. The ability of students to take their data from a fitness test and discover where they are in regard to healthy fitness zones promotes their health and lifetime learning and gives them the freedom to self-test and create their own fitness agenda. We do this by assessing baseline and posttraining fitness scores.

Power Standard 5

Student exhibits responsible personal and social behavior that respects self and others in physical activity settings.

KFO: I can play fairly.

The goal of this standard is the achievement of self-initiated behaviors that promote personal and group success in activity settings. These include safe practices, adherence to rules and procedures, etiquette, cooperation, teamwork, ethical behavior in sport, and positive social interaction. This standard develops respect for individual similarities and differences through positive interactions among participants in physical activity. We expect our students to be able to participate with all people, recognize the value of diversity in physical activity, and develop strategies for the inclusion of others.

This power standard is important because it gives teachers an accurate snapshot of who views activity positively and who views it negatively. We refer to this power standard as our *spirit of the game (SOTG)* standard. We view this standard in the affective domain, which encompasses students enjoying the activity and experiencing success. Because of this success and enjoyment, they come back to the activity. As we all know, active students can become active adults free of the debilitating diseases associated with inactivity. We believe that if students do not have fun, they probably won't return to the activity. The KFO for standard 5, "I can play fairly," refers to sportsmanship, fair play, and playing by the rules. In addition, this power standard refers to respecting oneself and others in physical activity. Self-officiating and including others in games and activities are also part of this standard.

We believe that standard 5 can go a bit deeper, looking at respect for the game or activity and enjoying it in a way that will motivate students to come back to it time and time again. That is the real goal of this power standard: enabling our students to enjoy activity so that they will return to it and become healthy, active adults. When assessing this power standard, we are looking at students in team and individual activities.

SOTG originated from the sport of Ultimate Frisbee. This particular sport requires that participants self-officiate, include others, and play by the rules of the game. We look at SOTG as the highest level of meeting standard 5. When students respect the game by playing the way it is meant to be played without officials, have fun in a safe and nurturing environment, and ultimately come back to the game again and again, then they have reached the highest level of this power standard. SOTG can also apply to fitness activities such as running, swimming, and so on—students learn to love these activities, participating for fun and for love of the activity.

Assessing the affective domain is a bit tricky. The affective domain is subjective in nature and objective assessment must be treated carefully so as not to contaminate the process with biased judgment. How do we know students are enjoying and participating in an activity in a positive manner? To objectify this standard, we have come up with our Pyramid of Active Participation (figure 2.1). It is composed of four levels and criteria of participation: Level 1 is what to do without the ball (just move, move to open space, be involved), level 2 is what to do with the ball (pass to a teammate, find an open teammate), level 3 is what students should be saying during activity (compliments and praise), and level 4, the highest level of participation, is teaching and helping others. Each of these levels is critical for the active participation of each student.

Level 1: Moving Without the Ball

This is the most basic level. The premise is that the participant needs to just move. When players do not move, the game slows down, and it is a frustrating experience for students who want to play the game. Often students simply have not been instructed on what to do in games. The first level of the pyramid assesses what students can do without a ball in activity settings. Just moving is at the center of this level. Listed here are behaviors that can be taught and assessed when moving without the ball:

- Just move.
- Get open.
- Be hard to guard.
- Move to the ball.
- Move to an open area.
- Play offense or defense.
- Use a V-cut to get open.

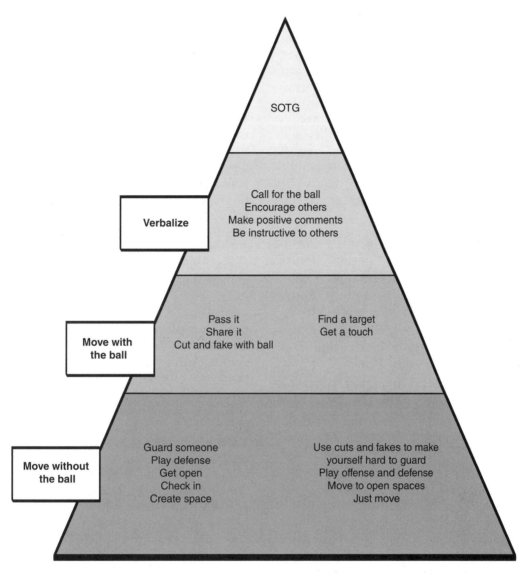

FIGURE 2.1 The Pyramid of Active Participation offers a way of understanding and assessing students' affective involvement in physical activity.

- Use an L-cut to get open.
- Use a curl cut to get open.
- Use a zigzag cut.
- Change running pace (fast, slow, jog, sprint, repeat).

Level 2: Moving With the Ball

The second level of the pyramid assesses what to do with the ball, such as pass it, find a target, share it, get a touch, make a move to get open and receive it, kick it, strike it, fake and go, and pass and cut. In order for students to be comfortable and make the game fun for others, we need to teach them what to do once the ball is in their possession. One way to assess this is to have students write down four or five types of movement that demonstrate that they understand what to do with the ball.

What to do with the ball:

- Find a target (to pass to).
- Look for a receiver.
- Pass it or share it.
- Pass and move.
- Pass and cut.
- Run with the ball.

Level 3: Positive Verbal Cues

The third level of the pyramid specifies what students can say in games to each other, such as giving compliments, sharing words of encouragement, calling out defensive or offensive directions, and verbally showing respect to each other.

As teachers, we need to model and have our students hear us using compliments, sharing words of encouragement, and showing respect for others. The more we quiz our students on what to say during activity, the sooner they will begin to talk and listen for these verbal cues of respect. Listed here are the positive, observable, and measurable verbal cues that we teach our students to say and listen for during games and activities:

- **Compliments:** "Jake, you really stayed with your mark."
- **Words of encouragement:** "Next time you'll make that catch, Katie." "Emily and Jessica, I like the way you run to the open space." "Nice job, Lindsay."
- **Calling out your defensive assignment or mark:** "I'm guarding Ryan."
- **Showing respect:** "Thank you." "Please." "Yes, Mrs. Summers." "May I help you with the equipment, Mr. Bert?"

Level 4: Spirit of the Game

Although we cannot truly assess what is going on inside the student's heads, we label this level as the top of the pyramid. If students know what to do without the ball, what to do with the ball, and what to say during activity, they have demonstrated SOTG in a physical education setting. The criteria in each level are general enough that they can apply to most, if not all, team sports and games.

We teach our students that this level comes from making the game fun for themselves and others, showing respect for equipment, playing in the true spirit of the game, showing respect for the game by following rules and putting forth effort, participating by moving at game speed, knowing what to do with the ball, knowing what to do without the ball, and playing offense and defense. This is the highest level of the pyramid, and when we see observable behaviors of the lower three levels, then by our definition, the students value activity. We teach and assess each level of the Pyramid of Active Participation and talk about the pyramid as a choice behavior, one that all students can show no matter the skill or fitness level. We look for and assess these levels in each of our units. Students who demonstrate

mastery of the first three levels will pass this standard, meeting the SOTG criteria.

Assessment of this standard largely takes place in a game situation. We like to assess this standard in small-sided games with special rules. Small-sided games allow teachers to put students into gamelike situations to maximize the number of times students can touch the ball. For example, we do not play 11-a-side soccer but will play 4-a-side soccer. When using small-sided games we also use short fields and courts because it is difficult to involve everyone on a full field such as in soccer. Four-a-side soccer requiring everyone to touch the ball (per side) before a shot is attempted, giving everyone a chance to touch the ball and practice skills in a game situation, is an example of a small-sided game with special rules. Another example of a small-sided game where everyone can touch the ball is playing 2v2 volleyball on badminton courts with a 7-foot (2 m) net. Many badminton standards have adjustable heights and can be used for volleyball, badminton, and pickleball. When the situation demands, we also play 3v3 volleyball. We call 2v2 and 3v3 volleyball *beach volleyball* because beach volleyball is played 2v2. Teaching and practicing skills in game situations enables students to learn the skills in the context of the actual game. Drilling students in long lines does not maximize time and equipment, is not gamelike, and is not fun!

Special rules in physical education include short fields or courts, small-sided games, requiring a certain number of passes until a shot is attempted, requiring everyone to touch the ball before a shot attempt, no goalies in small-sided soccer games, and short games with frequent rotations to play other teams. With small-sided games that involve goals, it is easy to substitute a cone or trash can as a goal, making it difficult to score. We do not use goalies because students often choose to be goalies in order to be sedentary. In addition, games using the rules of keep-away enable all students to be active and not be concerned with scoring goals. Keep-away is an excellent means to develop skills that involve moving without and with the ball.

Another problem that can occur with this standard is when students with mixed ability levels are playing together. This often leads to gender hogging (e.g., boys passing to only boys and girls passing only to girls) and friend hogging (two or three players dominating the game and excluding others). One way to combat this situation is to let students select the ability level of the game. For example, when using three soccer fields, the teacher names one field for beginners, another for intermediate players, and another for advanced players. Teachers can also name the fields *high school*, *college*, and *professional*. Additionally, we often have courts labeled *competitive* and *noncompetitive*.

A simple way to group students when some students are highly skilled and experienced is to use the highly skilled students as experts. Teachers can take a small group of students and group them with an expert, who assists with teaching the skill or serves as a passer in the small-group games. The highly skilled passers can make sure that everyone receives the ball in a game situation and can also give positive compliments and instructional cues to less experienced students. Students like to have a choice in games and activities. If we have previously taught soccer, Ultimate Frisbee, and speedball, for example, it is helpful to teach this standard by allowing students to choose to play on fields marked *soccer*, *Ultimate*, and *speedball*. When students are playing games they enjoy, teachers can put them into situations where they can best meet this standard. In short, give students a choice and a voice.

Again, when assessing this standard, we want students to feel successful, feel included, and have fun all at the same time. Students who experience all of these will likely come back to the activity and thereby engage in physical activity. In summary, here are the teaching situations that we put students in when we assess this standard:

- Small-sided games: 3v3, 4v4, keep-away
- Special rules: specified number of passes required, no goalies, modified goals (use of cones rather than goal nets)
- Student-chosen level of play: recreational, college, professional
- Shorter fields and small courts
- Frequent rotation of teams so that students play a variety of other students (lessens boredom and adds variety)
- Special groupings of students: random, selected by teacher, highly skilled grouped with unskilled and used as experts

We assess this standard using charts, quizzes, and checklists. Assessing with checklists involves tallying the number of times a student or teacher observes a particular criteria being demonstrated in a game setting. We use these assessment methods in five ways: (1) teachers use observation charts or checklists, (2) student partners use observation or checklist charts, (3) students check themselves regarding this standard, (4) teachers give in-class quizzes, and (5) teachers assign projects dealing with the Pyramid of Active Participation. We provide specific examples of this in chapter 8. All of our checklists involve the criteria in each level of the Pyramid of Active Participation: moving without the ball, moving with the ball, and what to say during games. Thus, by assessing this standard, we are actually assessing the Pyramid of Active Participation.

Learning Targets

- **Students apply SOTG in fitness activities, sport, and games.** SOTG is the goal of standard 5 and represents the pinnacle of the Pyramid of Active Participation. Teaching the facets of responsible and appropriate social behavior during sport and games is key. Being able to play fairly means students are socialized in positive experiences during physical activity outside and inside the school setting. All four levels of the pyramid are included with this learning target.

- **Students are able to self-officiate.** We put this learning target with this power standard in order to teach students to call their own fouls, miscues, and rule violations so that they can enjoy their participation and be able to keep playing without excessive interruption. If students cannot agree on a call, they should simply take turns in which team or person gets to make the call. Self-officiating is an important aspect of participation in sport and games outside the school setting. We want students to understand that the most important part of participation in games, sport, and fitness activities is not who wins and loses but enjoyment of the activity and continued participation in it.

- **Students demonstrate positive communication: praise, motivation, and encouragement.** Power standard 5 encompasses positive communication, praise, and encouragement with partners, teammates, and opponents so that students enjoy the activity, feel good about their participation, and choose to participate in the activity again and again. We teach students how to embrace positive communication so that others will enjoy the game and be motivated to keep participating.

- **Students demonstrate and sustain positive, active participation.** Building and drawing upon positive communication allows students to embrace, enjoy, and look forward to being active, an important facet of active participation. This learning target teaches students how to respect the game or activity so that they, their teammates, and their opponents will enjoy the game and feel good about being active in whatever physical activity they are engaged in.

Power Standard 6

Student chooses to live a healthy and fit life.

KFO: I value physical education, fitness, and health.

We need to teach students to appreciate that physical activity provides opportunities for enjoyment, challenge, self-expression, and social interaction. This standard is designed to develop an awareness of the intrinsic values and benefits of participation in physical activity.

The focus of this standard is what the students do outside of physical education class during leisure time. One can argue that valuing physical activity (chapter 9) and participating regularly (chapter 6) in physical activity are the same. Perhaps that is a good argument, but the main point is that we need to give our students the skills to regularly participate in physical activity and value being active. A study performed by Dr. Robert Pangrazi from Arizona State University showed that young people receive most of their daily physical activity outside of the school day (Morgan & Pangrazi, 2003). Students measured steps taken, and results demonstrated that they took approximately 1,500 steps per physical education class and 6,000 to 7,000 steps outside of class. In a similar study at Black Hills High School, student participation averaged 2,000 to 2,500 steps in each physical education class. Clearly, we need to teach students what they can do outside of the school day during leisure time.

Teaching students lifelong physical activity skills will enable them to lead a quality lifestyle. When their school careers are complete, students need to know what to do for physical activity and where to go to do it. We use a lot of self-reflection and personal-evidence-based assignments to help teach our students the skills necessary to achieve this.

The learning targets for this standard describe behaviors changed as a result of the learning experience (Siedentop, 1991). In other words, we want to know if what we taught in class is what our students value and apply outside of class. This is our ultimate goal: for students to value physical education and fitness during our classes but to also seek physical activity opportunities outside of our classroom.

Learning Targets

- **Students are able to find fitness and related activities in their community and other communities.** Physical educators need to teach students how to locate and access fitness and sport opportunities outside of school. We teach our students to explore opportunities such as local park and recreation departments, fitness events, fitness clubs, and city leagues.

- **Students motivate themselves and others toward fitness.** When students participate in fitness activities, many of them are more apt to do so with a friend, group class, or group of friends. We want students to know that fitness can be fun and motivating in the company of others and that they will return to the activity when it includes meaningful connections with others.

- **Students value setting goals and monitoring fitness progress and maintenance.** Setting personal fitness goals and self-assessing fitness levels is important for the overall health and well-being of students. Overtraining, injury, and burnout can be avoided when students understand how to set realistic and measurable personal fitness goals. By making fitness gains and losses observable through monitoring their progress, students can self-manage their personal fitness programs and seek the rewards of their progress.

- **Students actively engage in exercise, sport, and fitness.** By charting, logging, and recording steps, minutes, and types of activity, students will be able to see and feel the positive effects of physical exercise. Assessments included with this learning target focus on students recording their physical activity experiences so that being active will someday become a habit.

Summary

Now that we have taken a comprehensive look at each of the power standards, we hope you have an idea of their importance and their role in SBA. Chapter 3 will challenge each of us to prepare effective, research-based educational practices in the creation of formative and summative assessments. We will learn there is more to assessing students than just true–false tests, multiple-choice tests, or simple recall.

Standards-Based Assessment Strategies

Make each day your masterpiece.

—John Wooden

Using multiple methods of formative and summative assessments is critical to effective SBA. Further, using a variety of research-proven assessments provides the best opportunity to accurately measure students' knowledge, skill acquisition, and affective understanding. We have found success using the following research-based methods of assessment that we have adapted to physical education and our SBA system. Each assessment can be used either formatively or summatively.

Defining Formative and Summative Assessments

Both formative and summative assessments are key in determining the learning process of students and whether they have achieved the desired standards. Once again, we are learning if students have met, exceeded, or failed to meet the standards. *Formative assessments* allow the teacher to monitor the student's learning to ensure that learning gaps are filled and that achieving students are provided with enrichment opportunities to go more deeply into the learning. *Summative assessments* are given at a specific time to demonstrate what the student knows and does not know. Summative assessments can also help with the accountability of the student, teacher, district, and state.

Formative assessments are periodic assessments, such as quizzes. They align with power standards and learning objectives. Results are used to plan next steps, differentiate instruction, and provide feedback to students to improve their quality of work, improve understanding, and fill in any gaps or provide challenges through enrichment. Formative assessment provides teachers with the ongoing ability to diagnose and prescribe intervention and enrichment for students. A formative assessment is the process of checking students' understanding, allowing them to succeed or fail during the assessment with little to no risk. Teachers immediately learn which students need help, which students are ready to move on, and which students may need clarification of a standard, concept, unit, learning target, or objective. What we most appreciate about formative assessment is that it allows students to assess what they know (or do not know) without being graded on it. Students are not punished or rewarded for their learning rate. Formative assessment supports student learning by allowing teachers to vary instructional strategies and add time when necessary. Formative assessment is really about providing students time to practice.

Summative assessments, on the other hand, are typically given at a specific time when we feel students have demonstrated readiness in their formative assessments. Summative assessments are standardized tests, district tests, classroom-based assessments, unit tests, concept tests, and comprehensive assessments. Typically, summative assessments are part of our grading practices. Students receive a grade, teacher feedback, score, percentage, or rubric communicating whether or not they mastered the desired standard. Summative assessments often occur over longer periods of time, affording the teacher and student time to prepare and practice for the test.

We find it works best to give students opportunities for multiple formative assessments. Once again, we use a variety of research-based assessment methods, provide students with feedback on these assessments, and of course support students' specific needs in class. When our students demonstrate readiness (i.e., when they are successful in formative assessments), it is time to give them an opportunity to demonstrate standard achievement on a summative assessment.

Teachers who use SBA allow their students to be successful in formative assessments without the risk of damaging their grade. And when students are ready, these teachers have appropriately prepared them to be successful on a graded summative assessment.

Assessment Methods

In this section, we discuss the research-based teaching and assessment strategies that we use for our physical education assessments. Much of the teaching in physical education is centered on the psychomotor and the affective domains, but we can increase learning by also teaching and assessing in the cognitive domain. By assessing in the cognitive domain, we enhance students' analytical, creative, and evaluative thinking. The thinking skills of the cognitive domain are improved by providing students with opportunities for comparing, contrasting, analyzing, sequencing, and evaluating their work and that of others (Mitchell & Hutchinson, 2003). This gives students a truly comprehensive physical education experience.

Although asking students to do and to demonstrate is an important aspect of assessment in physical education, it is just as important to make sure students comprehend the meaning of the information we are teaching. Comprehension is the key to learning, and it is what we are assessing when we look at our cognitive concepts. We design written assessments that require students to organize information, understand relationships among variables, and demonstrate comprehension.

This chapter provides teachers with many evidence-based assessments that are proven to work in real-world physical education settings.

We provide specific examples of both formative and summative assessments in chapters 4 through 9. Here is a look at our assessment approaches.

Scaffolding

Scaffolding involves giving students prompts and hints to help them solve a problem or answer a question. This strategy enables teachers to assess what students have learned or not learned (Van Der Stuyf, 2002). Scaffolding facilitates a student's ability to build on prior knowledge and past lessons in order to internalize new information (Chang, Chen, & Sung, 2002). It enables students to learn more and more difficult material by progressing from the simple to the more difficult. By presenting cues and hints to students in a decreasing frequency, students are better able to internalize the information (Raymond, 2000). Scaffolding enables the learner to become more independent and a better self-regulating learner and problem solver (Hartman, 2002). Most important, the student is better able to complete the task and master the learning targets (Chang et al., 2002).

Scaffolding engages students in active learning. Instead of sitting and listening, the students are being prompted in the assessment of and building on previous knowledge and forming new knowledge (Van Der Stuyf, 2002). Additionally, there is evidence that scaffolding improves students' cognitive abilities (Ellis, Larkin, & Worthington, n.d.).

Formative assessments that employ scaffolding may be simple or difficult. For example, when assessing students' understanding of the fitness components, we have students circle the correct definition of each component from a list of four possible definitions. The correct definition is presented to them; they merely find the correct answer and circle it. In the next assessment, the students are asked to write the correct definition of the listed fitness components. And in the next assessment, students must list the fitness components and supply the correct definition for each. As scaffolding progresses, less information is provided, thereby increasing the difficulty.

Comparing and Contrasting

Identifying similarities and differences is a foundational mental operation that is basic to human thought (Gentner & Markman, 1994; Markman & Gentner, 1993a, 1993b; Medin, Goldstone, & Markman, 1995). When students are asked to identify similarities and differences, researchers have reported a 42%, 38%, and 46% improvement in test scores (Ross, 1988; Stahl & Fairbanks, (1986a). Working to identify similarities and differences enhances students' understanding and gives them the ability to use knowledge (Marzano, 2001). When students are identifying similarities and differences, they are engaging in metacognition, thereby comparing, classifying, and organizing information into bits of usable and comprehendible information (Santa, Havens, & Valdes, 2004). When students identify similarities and differences in graphic or symbolic form, their comprehension increases (Santa et al., 2004), thereby increasing their learning (Marzano, 2001).

We use comparing and contrasting especially in assessments related to the fitness components, FITT principle, and SPORT training principles. The teacher can first model this strategy by listing similarities and differences between two sports, such as tennis and badminton. They are both net sports and racket sports, and other similarities include rules, etiquette, singles and doubles, indoors and outdoors, and one hit per side. The differences include court size, net length and height, scoring, equipment, serving, and serving rotation.

This strategy can be accomplished in a variety of ways. It is our practice to identify similarities and differences using the following research-based strategies (Marzano, 2001):

- Venn diagrams
- Analogies
- Graphic organizers

Venn Diagrams

Venn diagrams are a visual tool for helping students to understand similarities and differences between concepts. Two intersecting circles are drawn that represent two concepts. The similarities between the concepts are listed in the space where the two circles intersect, while the differences are listed in the parts of the two circles that do not join together. For example, looking at the similarities and differences between muscular endurance and muscular strength using a Venn diagram has been a strategy that we have used with much success. Venn diagrams can also be used to compare two or three pieces of information, such as comparing and contrasting various sport rules, skills, and relationships between the fitness components and the FITT principle and SPORT training principles. Venn diagrams are described in some sources as graphic organizers. We have included them here because of our heavy emphasis on comparing and contrasting.

Analogies

Using analogies to illustrate two seemingly dissimilar relationships helps students to understand new information and increases student comprehension and learning (Alexander, 1984; Marzano, 2001; Ratterman & Gentner, 1998; Sternberg, 1997, 1979, 1978). Identifying similarities and differences is a higher level of thinking because it requires the learner to look at comparisons between relationships. For example, the teacher can ask students to compare the relationship between intensity and target heart rate with the relationship between intensity and lifting three sets of eight repetitions (i.e., both relationships are looking at how hard one should train when performing strength and cardiorespiratory workouts).

Graphic Organizers

Also called *nonlinguistic representations*, graphic organizers include charts, tables, lists, calendars, posters, and concept maps. Graphic organizers are an excellent learning tool because nonlinguistic learning (mental images, charts, pictographs) and linguistic learning (written statements) are both methods by which students store knowledge. Graphic organizers allow students to draw upon their mental images of what they know and to express this knowledge to demonstrate mastery of the content (Marzano, 2001). Graphic organizers also help students link new ideas together in a visual setting. They make thinking visible and help students organize, reorganize, revise, and modify the connections between new and existing ideas (Mitchell & Hutchinson, 2003). When we present small bits of material during our teaching progressions, students can use graphic organizers to connect ideas and see the relationships among the bits of information. Students who have difficulty putting their thoughts in writing often find it helpful to make a calendar, chart, or other graphic organizer. Venn diagrams, compare-and-contrast charts, and sequence maps are also examples of graphic organizers (Santa et al., 2004). These are valuable tools that enable students to demonstrate mastery in organizing information and relating to the teacher what they comprehend about the material (Marzano, 2001).

Self-Reflection

Self-reflection assessments allow students to draw upon their linguistic knowledge of content. Many students prefer this method to demonstrate mastery. In this case, they are making statements pertaining to what they remember (Marzano, 2001). Journals, logs, letters, book reviews, reports, essays, portfolios, and SMART goals are examples of self-reflection. As we will see later in this book, we use self-reflection in many of our summative assessments, often giving students the opportunity to use linguistic methods to demonstrate what they know.

Self-reflection summarizes what the student has performed or learned while engaging in an ongoing process, such as a one-month exercise analysis. Summarizing is a proven tool for demonstrating comprehension. It involves keeping, moving, deleting, and substituting information. When students learn to summarize, they increase their comprehension and recall (Raphael & Kirschner, 1985). When they are taught to delete some information, keep some information, and substitute information, their learning further improves (Anderson & Hidi, 1988).

Technological Devices

Technology has many uses in the physical education assessment process. For example, various devices can be used in formative assessments and serve as self-checks for students to gauge their intensity of physical activity. Pedometers, heart rate monitors, and accelerometers are examples of devices that students can use in assessing their heart rates, step counts, and speed. GPS devices are also becoming increasingly popular in physical education for geocaching.

Digital cameras are another useful device. For example, we take photos of students demonstrating movements or skills and then ask students to name basic biomechanical principles demonstrated in the pictures. This is an excellent way to check for understanding either as a review or as a closing activity.

Online homework assignments such as quizzes and fitness calculators are effective and easy, and they require little to no technological maintenance. Homework in physical education can extend learning and function as formative assessment, self-assessment, and summative assessment. In order for homework to be successful, the purpose of the assignment must be identified so that the students understand why they are doing it (Foyle, 1985; Foyle & Bailey, 1988; Foyle, Lyman, Tompkins, Perne, & Foyle, 1990). The homework needs to be centered on familiar content and prepare the student for new information (Marzano, 2001). In addition, when addressing physical education cognitive concepts, it may take up to 24 practice trials before students reach 80% competency (Anderson, 1995; Newell & Rosengloom, 1981). This further supports our assumption that assessing multiple times and providing multiple assessments is necessary to meet standards because this allows more practice trials using the material. Many of our assessments can be done at home. Using online fitness calculators is especially helpful to students because they can self-assess their fitness scores and write their fitness goals in the privacy of their own homes.

Direct Questioning and Response

We use direct questioning of students to check for understanding, gauge learning, and plan future lessons; in short, questioning is an excellent assessment tool. One way we use questioning is with students who have not mastered comprehension of the fitness concepts, FITT principle, and SPORT training principles. We walk up to students during activities and ask them to clarify their answers in case we cannot read their writing or feel that they need more attempts at the question in order to meet the standard (Bangert-Drowns, Kulik, & Kulik, 1992).

Questioning has a positive effect on student learning (Dempster, 1997; Dempster & Perkins, 1993; Hamaker, 1986; Richardson, 1985). Questioning can improve learning by up to 150% (Thalheimer, 2003). Questioning can be used in each level of Bloom's taxonomy: knowledge (recollection), comprehension, application, analysis, synthesis, and evaluation. (We'll discuss Bloom's taxonomy in more detail later in this chapter.) Asking questions gives students the chance to focus their attention and practice retrieving information (Nungester & Duchastel, 1980); repeats the learning material, which increases learning (Thalheimer, 2003); and motivates students because they feel good about their ability to retrieve information (Bjork, 1994; Glover, 1989).

As mentioned, questioning students gives students extra practice retrieving information, which increases learning up to 45% (Thalheimer, 2003). In addition, verbal questioning produces better results than written questions (Rothkopf & Bloom, 1970). We use a lot of questioning after we have given formative assessments regarding fitness concepts, the FITT principle, and the SPORT training principles.

Demonstrating

For students who do not perform well on cognitive assessments, we use assessments where we ask the student to show the teacher how to swing, kick, throw, and strike an implement using the five main biomechanical principles. We often ask all students to show the teacher the basic biomechanics of a skill because we do not have enough time to develop highly skilled performers. In addition, motor skill testing is limited by amount of practice time, genetic and environmental factors, and variations in normal growth and development (Pangrazi, 2005). In subsequent chapters, we discuss in detail how we assess motor skills.

Importance of Varied Assessment Methods

Long ago in our teacher education courses in college, we were introduced to Benjamin Bloom, who headed a group of educational psychologists in classifying levels of intellectual behavior important in learning. Bloom found that over 95% of the test questions students encounter require them to think only at the lowest possible level: recalling information.

Bloom identified six levels of learning in the cognitive domain, ranging from the simple recall or recognition of facts through increasingly more complex and abstract mental levels to the highest order, which is evaluation. Following are examples that represent intellectual activity on each level.

1. **Knowledge:** arrange, define, duplicate, label, list, memorize, name, order, recognize, relate, recall, repeat, reproduce, and state
2. **Comprehension:** classify, describe, discuss, explain, express, identify, indicate, locate, report, restate, review, select, and translate
3. **Application:** apply, choose, demonstrate, dramatize, employ, illustrate, interpret, operate, practice, schedule, sketch, solve, use, and write
4. **Analysis:** analyze, appraise, calculate, categorize, compare, contrast, criticize, differentiate, discriminate, distinguish, examine, experiment, question, and test
5. **Synthesis:** arrange, assemble, collect, compose, construct, create, design, develop, formulate, manage, organize, plan, prepare, propose, set up, and write
6. **Evaluation:** appraise, argue, assess, attach, choose, compare, defend, estimate, judge, predict, rate, select, support, value, and evaluate

Bloom's taxonomy helps us to keep in mind the varied ways our students learn and retain knowledge. In a typical classroom setting, students are usually involved only passively in learning (e.g., listening to the instructor, looking at the occasional overhead or slide, reading textbooks). Research shows that such passive involvement generally leads to a limited retention of knowledge. According to Ronald A. Berk in his book, *Professors Are From Mars, Students Are From Snickers*, (2003), the only way to get 100% retention of information is by "hearing, seeing, doing, smelling, feeling, tasting, inhaling, injecting and purchasing on credit" (Berk, 2003, pp. 48-52).

However, research also indicates that by reorganizing or adapting the ways they present material to students, instructors can create an environment in which knowledge retention is significantly increased. Of course, such situations require the cooperation of the students themselves.

One of the best methods is to implement active learning, or involve students directly and actively in the learning process itself. This means that instead of simply receiving information verbally and visually, students are receiving, participating, and doing. In simple terms, then, active learning is,

according to the Dunn learning style model, engaging students in doing something besides listening to a lecture and taking notes to help them learn and apply course material. Students may be involved in talking and listening to one another, or writing, reading and reflecting individually. (Dale, 1969, p. 42)

A process we use in the classroom is collaborative learning, which is

a subset of active learning activities that engage students in interacting with one another while learning and applying the information. Usually it involves breaking the class into small groups (of 2 or 3 students) and us posing a question, often of a conceptual nature, and allowing each group to discuss a possible answer for a period of a minute or two. We then seek answers at random. (Dale, 1969, p. 42)

Note that students sitting in a group and studying together, or group projects in which only one or two students do all the work, do not constitute active or collaborative learning.

Summary

What can we learn from research-based assessments? We can remind ourselves that assessments can and should be so much more than true–false, multiple-choice, fill-in-the-blank, and short-answer questions. We can borrow assessment ideas from leading researchers and practicing teachers. We cannot use the excuse that it doesn't work in physical education; we have tested all of the ideas discussed earlier in this chapter and they do work. These assessment strategies challenge our students and check their depth of understanding. If our ultimate goal is for students to have the knowledge, values, and skills to lead a healthy and fit life, we need to make sure our assessments accurately assess their comprehension, application, and ability to self-evaluate.

Again, as we develop and create assessments we need to keep in mind the various types of assessments, degree of higher-level learning, and processes by which our students learn. Are we only assessing students their recollection of information, or are we challenging them to know, comprehend, apply, analyze, synthesize, and evaluate?

Part II is the practical part of this book. In it, we describe how to assess the power standards, and we provide formative and summative assessments for specific learning targets. We explain the type of assessments used and how to set them up. This book and the assessments in it will help you to develop physically educated students that meet or exceed standards.

Using Power Standards

CHAPTER 4

Power Standard 1: I Can Move Correctly

A winner is someone who recognizes his God-given talents, works his tail off to develop them into skills, and uses these skills to accomplish his goals.

—Larry Bird

Power standard 1: Student demonstrates competency in motor skills and movement patterns needed to perform a variety of physical activities.

KFO 1: I can move correctly.

Learning targets

- Students can identify and apply five biomechanical principles of human movement: opposition, weight transfer, torque, tracking, and follow-through.
- Students are able to discuss, evaluate, and assess common strategies in sport and games.

ASSESSMENT FORMS

Formative Assessments

- Biomechanics 1: Connect the Dots
- Biomechanics 2: Identify the Principle (figures 4.1-4.10)
- Biomechanics 3: Skill Scaffolding (forms 4.1-4.4)
- Biomechanics 4: Metacognition (form 4.5)
- Biomechanics 5: Identifying the Correct Answer (forms 4.6-4.7)
- Biomechanics 6: Biomechanical Principle Motor Skills Assessment (forms 4.8-4.9)
- Biomechanics 7: Similarities and Differences (forms 4.10-4.13)
- Biomechanics 8: Class Checklist (form 4.14)
- Biomechanics 9: Self- and Peer Evaluation (form 4.15)
- Biomechanics 10: Weight Training (form 4.16)
- Sport Strategies Before-and-After T-Chart (form 4.17)
- Sport Strategies Compare and Select (form 4.18)

Summative Assessments

- Biomechanics of Human Movement Project (form 4.19)
- Graphic Organizer: Yoga Bingo (forms 4.20-4.21)
- Graphic Organizer: Biomechanical Principle Bingo (forms 4.22-4.23)
- I Can Move Correctly: Self-Reflection (form 4.24)

Posters

- Biomechanics of Human Movement (form 4.25)
- Kid-Friendly Biomechanics (form 4.26)
- Common Strategies in Sport and Games to Increase Offensive and Defensive Success (form 4.27)
- Five Ball-Control Methods of Racket Sports: Problem Solving on the Court (form 4.28)

The goal of this standard is the development of movement competence and proficiency. We want students to develop and sustain movement competence by applying biomechanical principles of human movement and common sport strategies. So how do we go about doing this? We direct our instruction toward the two learning targets of this power standard: biomechanical principles and common strategies in sport and games.

We start by teaching the biomechanical principles of opposition, weight transfer, tracking, torque, and follow-through. We have found great success in identifying the biomechanics of movement for each motor skill and activity we teach. Whether we are teaching Ultimate Frisbee, tennis, or golf, as we explain the skills, we also demonstrate the biomechanical principles behind them. We want each student to be able to identify, explain, apply, and analyze these biomechanical principles for a variety of activities. We find that by teaching the five biomechanical principles, our students' skill acquisition improves. By helping students understand how to move correctly, we continually observe skill transfer and self-correction of errors.

Our second learning target, teaching common strategies in sport and games, teaches students to be competent in the comprehension and application of fundamental offensive and defensive tactics. We focus on offensive and defensive strategies, what to do when you have possession, what to do when you lose possession, and what each player's role can be. These strategies help students to be successful in the sports and games that we teach. We want our students to have the confidence to join games and sports with the offensive and defensive philosophies to do well.

These learning targets help our students successfully meet and exceed power standard 1. Students learn motor skills and movement patterns that allow them to perform a variety of physical activities and to achieve a degree of success that makes the activities enjoyable.

Our success depends on the intentional use of appropriate and effective teaching strategies. Our formative and summative assessments are part of this. These assessments are user-friendly (for both teacher and student) templates to help build proficiency of skills through teaching the biomechanical principles. In this chapter, we provide the formative and summative assessment methods and tools that help our students demonstrate they have met standard 1 (KFO: "I can move correctly").

Formative Assessments

Using technique photos and colored stickers (such as those used to mark garage-sale prices) to identify landmarks on the body can help students better understand biomechanical principles of movement. These visual aids emphasize an aspect of human movement, which helps students break information into manageable pieces to absorb. For example, stickers can be placed on the body to help a student visualize where a ball needs to make contact on the body, how to perform a follow-through, and the abstract concepts of opposition, weight transfer, and body alignment to target. The first two formative assessments (Biomechanics 1 and 2) explain how we use these aids in our classes to teach biomechanical principles.

Biomechanics 1: Connect the Dots

Provide dot stickers such as those used to mark garage-sale prices. Each student should have two stickers to place on the appropriate body targets. These stickers serve as visual landmarks as we teach the follow-through for these four skills:

- Tennis forehand—The student is playing tennis and is right-handed. Put one sticker under the right wrist and one on the left shoulder. As the student swings, he connects the dots on the follow-through: The right wrist makes near contact with the dot on the left shoulder, thus connecting the dots.

- Tennis serve—The student is playing tennis and is right-handed. Put one sticker under the right wrist and one on the left hip. As the student serves, she connects the dots on the follow-through.

- Volleyball serve—The student is performing an overhead serve and is right-handed. Place one dot under the right wrist and one on the right knee. As the student swings, he connects the dots on the follow-through.

- Overhand throw—The student is throwing a ball and is right-handed. Put one sticker under the right wrist and one on the side of the left hip. As the student throws, she connects the dots on the follow-through.

Biomechanics 2: Identify the Principle

Using a camera, sport magazines, or sport section of the newspaper, take or find pictures that illustrate the biomechanical principles. Number them and have students write down the biomechanical principles that are shown. Select pictures from one activity or many. It is great to use pictures of students or the student-athletes who make the sport section.

The student could see a photo like figure 4.1 and write the following:

FIGURE 4.1 What biomechanical principles are evident in this student's movement?

1. This is tracking—I see the player looking down at the ball she is about to strike.

2. This is weight transfer—As she swings her leg, it goes from a behind position to a forward position.

3. This is torque—I see the player's hips open up, twisting and turning toward the target as she swings her leg.

4. This is stepping in opposition—her planted foot is forward while her opposing arm is back. She is also planting with the left foot and kicking with the right.

Figures 4.2-4.10 are some other examples of how technique photos can demonstrate biomechanical principles.

FIGURE 4.2 Balance and ready position.

FIGURE 4.3 Opposition; sideways (left-handed).

FIGURE 4.4 Stepping in opposition.

FIGURE 4.5 Tracking, weight transfer, and stepping in opposition (right-handed).

FIGURE 4.6 Weight transfer; weight follows Frisbee (right-handed).

FIGURE 4.7 Tracking—eye on the ball.

FIGURE 4.8 Tracking—eye on the Frisbee.

FIGURE 4.9 Torque—turn hips and shoulders and follow through.

FIGURE 4.10 Weight transfer, torque, and stepping in opposition.

Here are some other great formative assessments using pictures of people performing biomechanical principles:

1. Number the pictures and have students correctly write the principle for each picture (e.g., quiz, pair share, station sheet). Provide pictures of the activity students are currently engaged with or pictures of several activities.

2. Have students take pictures of each other to demonstrate specific principles (e.g., "At station 3, I want you to take a picture of stepping in opposition for the overhead throw, and I want you to take a picture of torque."). At the end of the class, look through the digital photos and assess whether the students were able to demonstrate the principles correctly.

3. Include photos featuring biomechanical errors and have students explain why they are incorrect and how to correct them, such as a picture of a young girl leaning backward and throwing a football with the same stepping leg as her throwing arm. A student who understands opposition and weight transfer should be able to accurately describe the errors and correct them.

The goal is for students to know and be able to apply these five biomechanical principles. We need to assess them through various evidence-based methods. First we use pictures and landmarks to teach these concepts. Once students are familiar with the terminology and definitions of the biomechanical principles, we then check student understanding through formative cognitive assessments. Forms 4.1 through 4.24 are examples of these cognitive assessments. Each assessment gets progressively more difficult. As with Bloom's taxonomy, the students start with basic knowledge of the biomechanical principles that they can recall, which we further develop by having students analyze biomechanical principles through pictures, peer assessments, and self-assessments. Students refine the application of these biomechanical principles through various skills and movements, which then leads to the highest level of thinking, teaching the biomechanical principles to oneself and others. Following are the formative assessments we have developed to lead to student success.

Biomechanics 3: Skill Scaffolding

Forms 4.1 through 4.4 begin the scaffolding assessments. In the first assignment, form 4.1, students are presented with five biomechanical principles and three possible definitions for each, and they must circle the best definition for each one. Students will recognize, recall, and select the correct answer from the information that is provided. This graphic organizer is a great way to help students begin to categorize each principle with the correct definition.

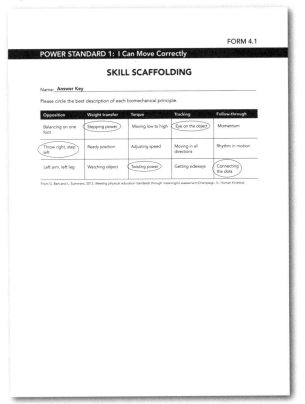

Form 4.2 identifies the correct definition of each biomechanical principle and omits critical information (the name of the correct biomechanical principle). Students demonstrate knowledge of the biomechanical principles by choosing the correct biomechanical principle that matches the supplied definition.

Form 4.3 requires students to recall, identify, choose, and apply both the names of the biomechanical principles and the correct definitions. With this form, students are assessed on the first three levels of Bloom's taxonomy: knowledge (recall), comprehension (identify), and application (apply and choose).

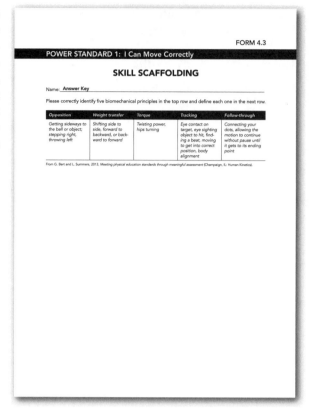

In form 4.4, the kinesthetic-psychomotor domain is assessed. Students perform a skill in front of the teacher, who notes whether each biomechanical principle is being performed correctly or incorrectly and provides written feedback in each box that will help the student improve. For example, if the teacher is assessing several students simultaneously on the tennis forehand swing, the teacher may simply use a check minus, check, or check plus to indicate the level of proficiency or mastery achieved. This may help alleviate the time involved in providing feedback to each student. We suggest providing feedback to each student but once again time along with the number of students needs to also be a factor in considering provided feedback.

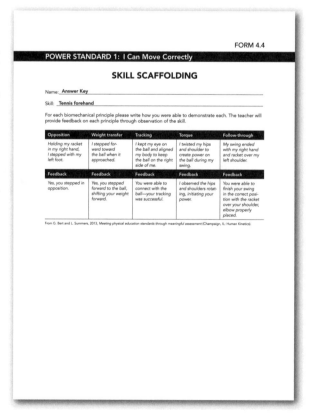

Biomechanics 4: Metacognition

This is an example of the highest level of scaffolding. In form 4.5, critical-thinking skills such as synthesis, analysis, and evaluation of information are used as students write about the relationships between the biomechanical principles and the five fitness components. In this example, students are analyzing the fitness benefits of playing tennis and giving examples of using a tennis skill with a particular biomechanical principle. In addition, open-ended questions are used to make students evaluate and appraise information that has been presented in class. Remember that we provide only examples of answers to the open-ended questions; there may be many other possible answers. This is the benefit of open-ended questioning—it gives students the chance to use various critical-thinking skills and to think creatively.

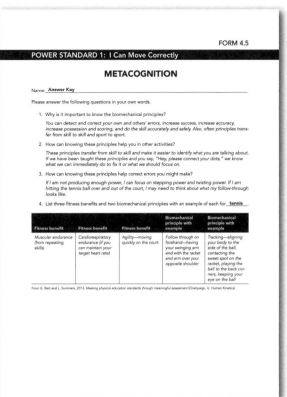

Biomechanics 5: Identifying the Correct Answer

Form 4.6 assesses knowledge and comprehension of the five biomechanical principles as they relate to tennis. This graphic organizer presents students with five biomechanical principles and a choice of three possible definitions for each, and they are asked to circle the best definition. Students will recognize, recall, and select information.

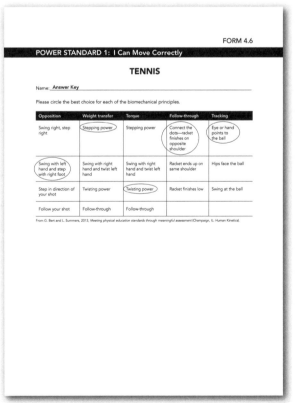

Form 4.7 is a graphic organizer that assesses knowledge and comprehension of the five biomechanical principles as they relate to soccer. It presents students with five biomechanical principles and a choice of three possible definitions and asks them to circle the best definition for each principle. Students will recognize, recall, and select information.

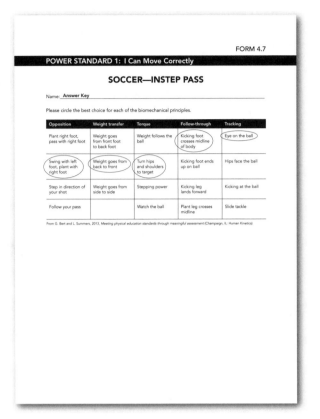

Biomechanics 6: Biomechanical Principle Motor Skills Assessment

Form 4.8 is a checklist that we use to assess tennis. This checklist can be used by teachers, peers, and students themselves for self-assessment. The best approach is to pair students off and have partners assess each other. Another approach uses small groupings of three students each, one to perform the skill, another to assess and write an *X* or minus (–), and a third to toss the ball, retrieve, or count. This assessment measures the forehand groundstroke, backhand groundstroke, and overhead serve in tennis.

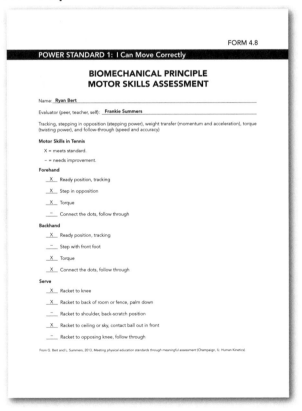

Form 4.9 is a pre- and post testing assessment using a checklist format for the forehand groundstroke. Here, we are assessing the ready position, backswing, swing, contact point, follow-through, and the three ball controls. Use an *X* for meeting a standard and a minus sign (–) for not meeting the standard or not showing any visible sign of using a particular criteria.

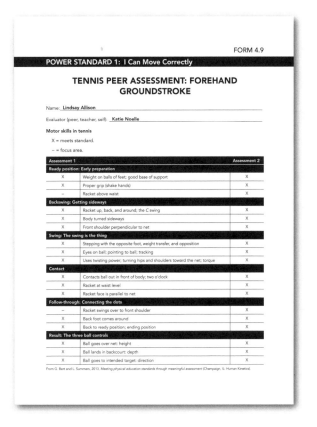

Biomechanics 7: Similarities and Differences

Many of the biomechanical principles are similar and therefore can transfer to many skills. For example, throwing a ball has similar movements to the tennis serve. Are students able to see these similarities and are they also able to see how the movements are different? Using Venn diagrams helps students to visually categorize these similarities and differences.

An example of a Venn diagram is shown in figure 4.11.

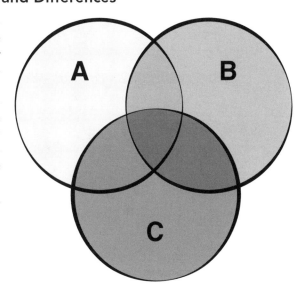

FIGURE 4.11 Venn diagrams show similarities and differences.

The next forms show sample assessments using Venn diagrams. Venn diagrams are an excellent strategy for comparing and contrasting similarities and differences.

Form 4.10 compares and contrasts throwing a ball and the tennis serve. Throwing a ball is often a lead-up activity to teaching the tennis serve. The areas outside of the intersection will be used to list differences, and the area where both circles intersect is used to list the similarities.

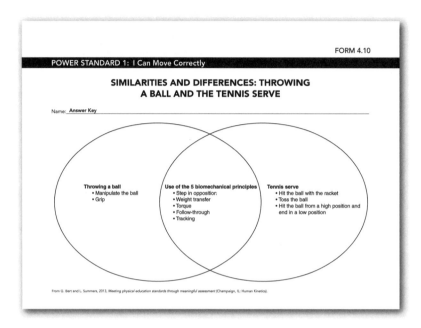

Form 4.11 compares and contrasts the golf swing and baseball swing.

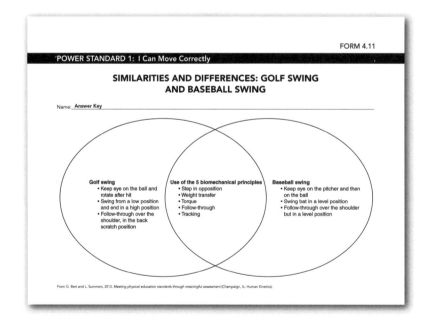

Form 4.12 compares and contrasts the biomechanical principles of weight transfer and stepping in opposition.

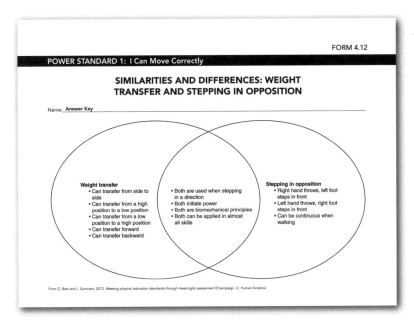

Form 4.13 looks at offense and defense.

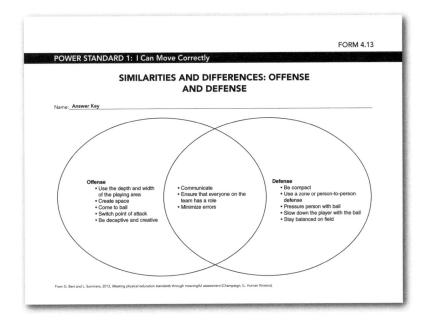

Biomechanics 8: Class Checklist

Form 4.14 is an all-class checklist with rows for multiple student names. The teacher can use it to assess in mass or in small groups as students engage in a skill using all five biomechanics.

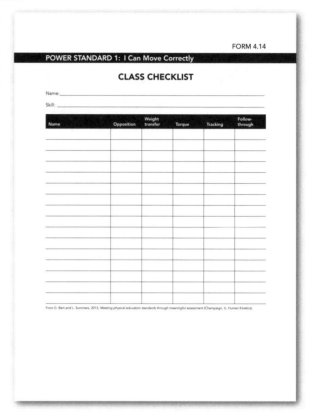

FORM 4.14

POWER STANDARD 1: I Can Move Correctly

CLASS CHECKLIST

Name:_____

Skill: _____

Name	Opposition	Weight transfer	Torque	Tracking	Follow-through

From G. Bert and L. Summers, 2013, *Meeting physical education standards through meaningful assessment* (Champaign, IL: Human Kinetics).

Biomechanics 9: Self- and Peer Evaluation

Form 4.15 assesses the biomechanics of throwing. In this example, students work in pairs and assess each other in each phase of throwing. Students simply place a mark in the correct column (met standard or continue working). We are asking students to recognize and observe the biomechanical principles of themselves and others when throwing a ball.

FORM 4.15

POWER STANDARD 1: I Can Move Correctly

SELF- AND PEER EVALUATION

Throwing accuracy	Name: *Joe Meyer*		Partner name: *Natalie Brown*	
	Met standard	Continue working	Met standard	Continue working
Stand sideways to target.	X			X
Step with front foot with opposition.	X			X
Transfer weight back to front.	X			X
Bend throwing arm to 90°.	X		X	
Generate twisting power from torque.	X		X	
Follow through to opposite thigh.	X		X	

From G. Bert and L. Summers, 2013, *Meeting physical education standards through meaningful assessment* (Champaign, IL: Human Kinetics).

Biomechanics 10: Weight Training

How do the biomechanical principles look in fitness classes? Many physical educators are not only teaching sport and games but fitness too. Form 4.16 provides an example of how you could approach teaching and assessing the biomechanical principles in a weightlifting class. It directs students to circle the best weightlifting technique for the bench press, parallel squat, and leg press. In addition, knowledge of fitness components is assessed, looking at the differences between muscle endurance and strength.

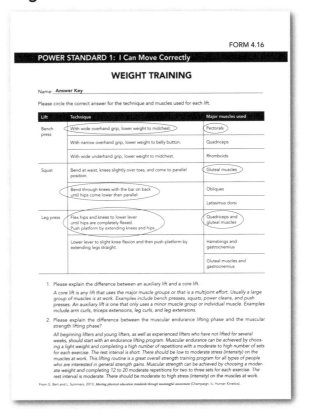

Sport Strategy Assessments

How do you explain how to play offense and defense? Students don't magically walk into class understanding the tactics and strategies of the sports we play; it is our job to teach and assess these. To start, we like to ask our students what they know about offensive and defensive strategies by brainstorming a list (see form 4.17). We find it is best to use a T-chart (both before and after we have taught these strategies). Few of our students have cognitive comprehension of what to do to maintain or get possession or what to do when they lose possession. Let's put it this way—their before list is short and often blank. Take a look at form 4.27 to get an idea of strategies that are common among all sports. This is a good starting point. After we have explained these strategies and asked students to apply them in sport, we then complete form 4.17 with the offensive and defensive strategies that they understand and can apply.

Also, you can give students a strategy and have them choose whether it is an offensive strategy, defensive strategy, or both. Our next assessment (form 4.18) checks just that. We give seven examples and students determine which strategy they fall under.

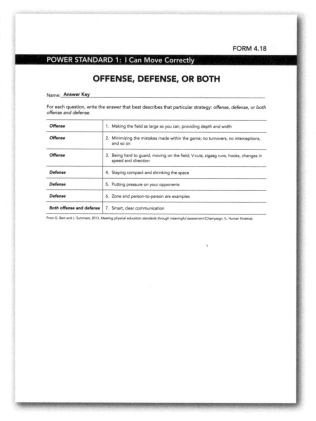

Additionally, you may choose to use a Venn diagram as previously discussed in figure 4.11 or another assessment method.

We have found that most physical educators do not teach these strategies and are often frustrated when a team or individual players dominate activities. Power standard 1 supports helping students to develop their technical skills and their tactical understanding of sport and games.

Summative Assessments

When our students have demonstrated comprehension of the biomechanical principles and common strategies in sport, it is time to test them through summative assessments. At this point, students should easily meet and exceed the standard on these summative assessments. As teachers, we know that our students know the material because we have checked understanding multiple times through various formative assessments, provided help for those lacking skills and knowledge, and provided support and feedback to all. These examples of summative assessments demonstrate that students have the skills and knowledge to move correctly, meaning they can identify, explain, and apply the biomechanical principles and common strategies in various physical activities. For each of these summative assessments, we keep exemplary work to provide students with strong examples each year.

Form 4.19 shows a summative assignment that is performed outside of class. Students are asked to find photos of the biomechanical principles. These can be self-portraits, drawings, or clippings from newspapers and magazines. Students must clearly identify and define each of the biomechanical principles. They can select one physical activity or several. This is a fun assessment that keys into the creative and artistic intelligence of students. Intellectual behaviors important for learning are assessed through synthesizing and analyzing biomechanical principles found in real-world situations. Through the years, we have assessed creative posters, collages, and even mobiles.

This is a favorite! Yoga Bingo is a wonderful assessment. Students are given a blank Yoga Bingo card (form 4.20) and a list of 30 yoga poses (form 4.21). They need to select 16 poses for their bingo card and draw or find a picture of each one. Students will submit their yoga cards before playing. These cards are graded on correctly identifying the poses in the pictures and the names of the poses.

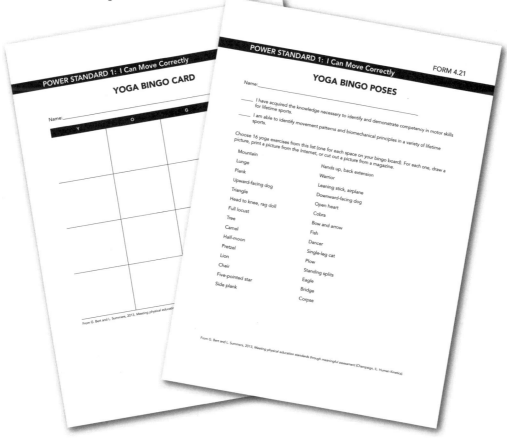

Now the fun part begins: playing Yoga Bingo. Each player chooses one bingo board and 16 chips (we cut up colored paper into small pieces). The teacher has all 32 poses written on 32 cards. The teacher shuffles the cards, places them facedown on the floor, and turns over a card. The teacher reads the card, for example, "Tree pose." All students perform the tree pose for the designated amount of time, approximately 20 seconds. Before the teacher turns over a new card, students place a chip on their yoga board if their board includes the tree pose. The game continues until a student has covered four spaces in a row vertically, horizontally, or diagonally. The first student to do this says, "Yoga!" Continue play until all cards have been turned over. Students are assessed on their board and poses.

Forms 4.22 and 4.23 are for a game we call *Movement Bingo*. The same rules and guidelines apply as in Yoga Bingo. The teacher calls out a movement principle and students pantomime a sport skill using the movement principle. For example, the teacher calls out "Weight transfer" and students perform the tennis forehand, stepping with the correct foot using weight transfer.

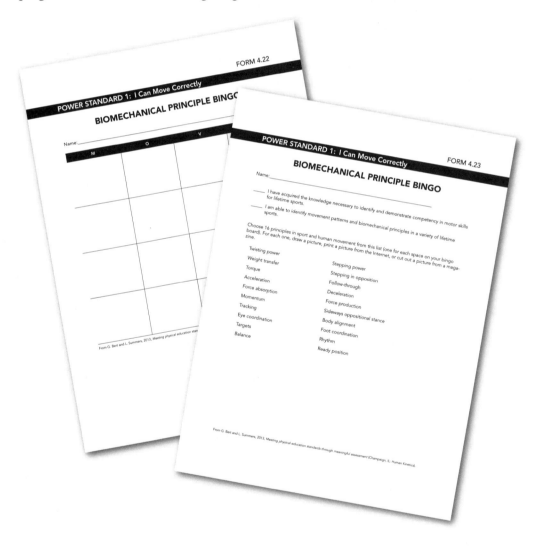

Form 4.24 is a summative assessment in the form of an end-of-term essay. It requires that students compose, defend, and argue their point of view in writing as to how they meet power standard 1 (KFO: "I can move correctly"). They must write about their knowledge and application of the five biomechanical principles, sport-specific skills (skills we have learned and refined), and movement concepts in games and sport (offensive and defensive strategies). This is a wonderful self-evaluation and reflection of whether they feel they have met power standard 1.

Posters

We post these information charts and visual aids on our walls, enlarging them to poster size. These examples illustrate the language and terminology we use when teaching these learning targets. We also provide these posters on our teacher webpage, which can help parents become familiar with the material taught in class and can be a great resource for students who miss class or need help.

Form 4.25 is a template of a poster that we put up in the teaching spaces at our school regarding biomechanics of human movement. We have listed eight biomechanics here.

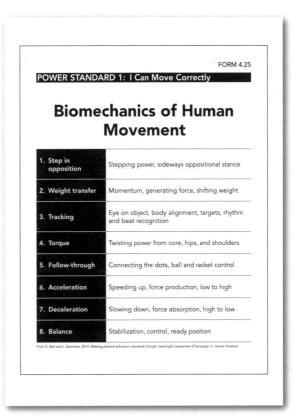

Form 4.26 is a template of a poster that we put up in the teaching spaces at our school. It lists student-friendly definitions of our five biomechanics.

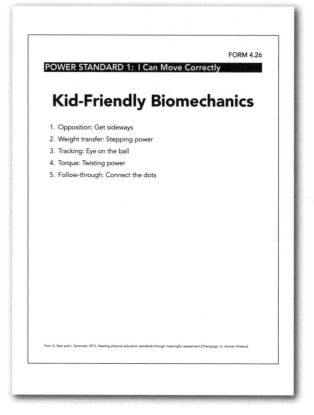

Form 4.27 is another template that can be made into a poster. It explains common strategies used in the lifetime sports that we teach. These concepts are basic offensive and defensive principles.

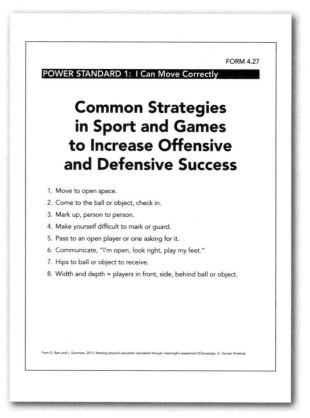

Form 4.28 is a template for a poster of basic ball controls used primarily in tennis.

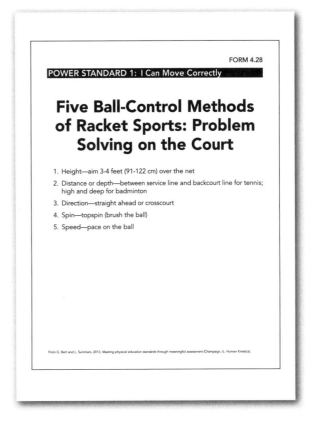

CHAPTER 5

Power Standard 2: I Can Train Myself and Others

Physical fitness is not only one of the most important keys to a healthy body; it is the basis of dynamic and creative intellectual activity.

—John Fitzgerald Kennedy

Power standard 2: Student is able to create and implement a fitness plan according to body-type needs, goals, and fitness maintenance.

KFO: I can train myself and others.

Learning targets

- Students understand, apply, and appreciate the components of physical fitness: cardiorespiratory endurance, muscular endurance, muscular strength, flexibility, and body composition.
- Students know and value the physical, mental, and social benefits of vigorous exercise and physical activity.
- Students show mastery of the FITT and SPORT training principles to design physical activity and sport training programs.

ASSESSMENT FORMS

Formative Assessments

- Fitness Components 1: Concept Scaffolding (forms 5.1-5.8)
- Fitness Components 2: Graphic Organizer (form 5.9)
- Fitness Components 3: Compare and Contrast (form 5.10)
- Fitness Components 4: Analogies (form 5.11)
- Benefits of Exercise 1: Concept Mapping (form 5.12)
- Benefits of Exercise 2: Graphic Organizer (form 5.13)
- SPORT Principles 1: Concept Scaffolding (form 5.14)
- SPORT Principles 2: Story (form 5.15)
- SPORT Principles 3: Daily Scenario (form 5.15)
- FITT Principles 1: Concept Scaffolding (forms 5.16-5.17)
- FITT Principles 2: Compare and Contrast (form 5.18)
- FITT and SPORT Principles: Checklists (forms 5.19-5.20)
- Exertion Levels: Pictures (form 5.21)

Summative Assessments

- FITT Project (forms 5.22-5.24)
- I Can Train Myself and Others: Self-Reflection (form 5.25)
- State test of health and fitness (not included, but we see it as a summative assessment)

Posters

- FITT Principle (form 5.26)
- SPORT Training Principles (form 5.27)
- Five Fitness Components of a Physically Educated Person (form 5.28)

One way in which physical education has changed and developed over the years has been the emphasis on cognitive concepts taught, understood, and applied to physical fitness. Effective assessment methods and teaching practices help us to emphasize these cognitive concepts and ensure that our students are learning. The second power standard emphasizes learning in the cognitive domain, and meeting the standard requires mastering the foundational fitness education concepts reflected in the learning targets.

The three learning targets used to teach this standard help students to learn about, maintain, and improve their overall physical fitness. They are used for long-range planning of fitness goals and represent an intentional approach to fitness improvement and sustainability.

How do we go about teaching and assessing these learning targets? We first want to make sure students understand what it means to be physically fit by teaching the five fitness components: cardiorespiratory endurance, muscular strength, muscular endurance, flexibility, and body composition. We want students to be able to identify each component, explain it, and provide examples. The fitness components are critical skills used for fitness planning and the pursuit of long-range fitness goals. All five are necessary for a person to be healthy and physically fit.

The second learning target is for students to comprehend and appreciate the physical, mental, and social benefits of exercise. We want them to understand, for example, why it is important to be flexible, what health gains one might see from improving fitness test scores, and how activity has a positive effect on mood. Students will approach exercise from a variety of perspectives. Some may choose to exercise for the physical benefits, while others will simply exercise in order to socialize with friends. For whatever reason students choose to exercise, they need to understand the various benefits so that they may internalize the need to exercise and gain the resulting benefits.

Finally, once students understand the components of fitness and benefits of exercise, we move to training principles, teaching and assessing FITT (frequency, intensity, time, and type) and SPORT (specificity, progression, overload, reversibility, and tedium). The FITT principle is a way for students to develop deeper understanding of each fitness component. It allows students to apply each of the fitness components and is a key element in organizing a fitness plan. The FITT principle is also a means by which students can learn to assess their own fitness goals. Self-assessment and self-planning are key to lifelong fitness. Whereas the FITT principle usually applies to individual fitness components, the SPORT training principles are used in conjunction with the FITT principle and other sports. The SPORT training principles allow students to more deeply analyze, plan, and apply an exercise and physical activity plan. We want students to be able to explain, compare, apply, and analyze FITT and SPORT so that they may use these principles with their daily training in class, create their own fitness plans, and be able to develop fitness plans for other people.

In order for us to know if our students have met these learning targets, we need to check their understanding throughout our teaching and instruction. We need to assess what they know and what they do not know. Following are the methods and tools of the formative and summative assessments that help our students demonstrate they have met standard 2, "I can train myself and others."

Formative Assessments

Fitness Components 1: Concept Scaffolding

Students have been taught the fitness component of cardiorespiratory endurance with regard to the FITT principle. In form 5.1, students first give the definition of cardiorespiratory endurance and then identify the correct answer from four that are given for each element of the FITT principle.

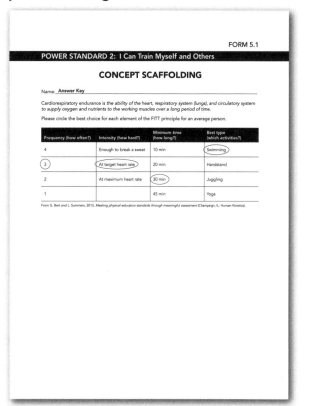

In form 5.2, we are now asking the student to define cardiorespiratory endurance as well as provide correct examples of the FITT principles. This is more challenging than form 5.1.

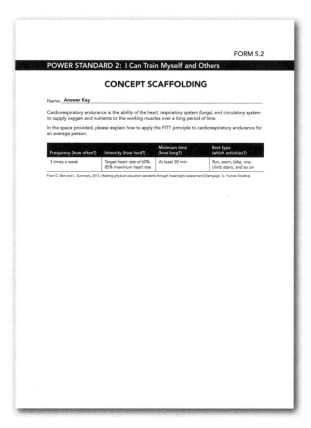

Students have been taught the fitness component of muscular endurance with regard to the FITT principle. In form 5.3, students first give the definition of muscular endurance and then identify the correct answer from four that are given for each element of the FITT principle.

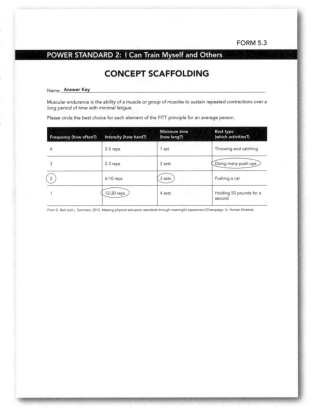

In form 5.4, we are now asking students to define muscular endurance as well as provide correct examples of the FITT principle. This is more challenging than form 5.3.

Students have been taught the fitness component of muscular strength with regard to the FITT principle. In form 5.5, students first give the definition of muscular strength and then identify the correct answer from four that are given for each element of the FITT principle.

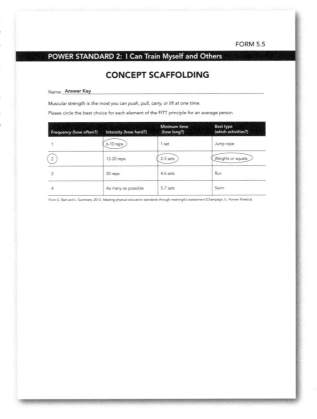

In form 5.6, we are now asking students to define muscular strength as well as provide correct examples for each element of the FITT principle. This is more challenging than form 5.5.

Students have been taught the fitness component of flexibility with regard to the FITT principle. In form 5.7, students first give the definition of flexibility and then identify the correct answer from four that are given for each element of the FITT principle.

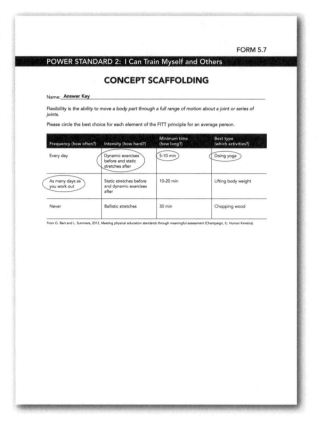

Form 5.8 now asks students to define flexibility as well as provide correct examples of each element of the FITT principle. This is more challenging than form 5.7.

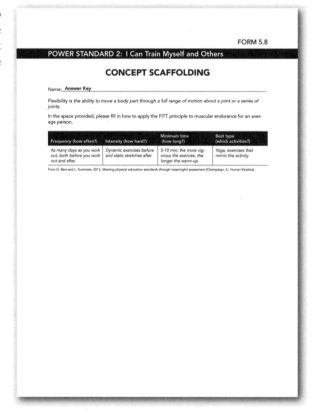

Fitness Components 2: Graphic Organizer

Students have been taught all five of the fitness components: cardio-respiratory endurance, muscular endurance, muscular strength, flexibility, and body composition. Form 5.9 is a graphic organizer for students to recall and explain answers about the components.

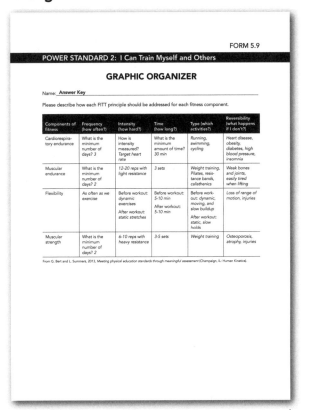

Fitness Components 3: Compare and Contrast

Form 5.10 is a Venn diagram. Oftentimes students have difficulty distinguishing between the two similar yet different fitness components of muscular strength and muscular endurance. The Venn diagram cognitively organizes these two fitness components.

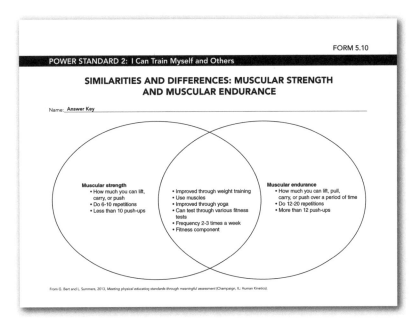

Fitness Components 4: Analogies

In form 5.11, we have used analogies to help assess training principles and fitness components. This is a great higher-level-thinking tool for assessing the connections students have made with these concepts.

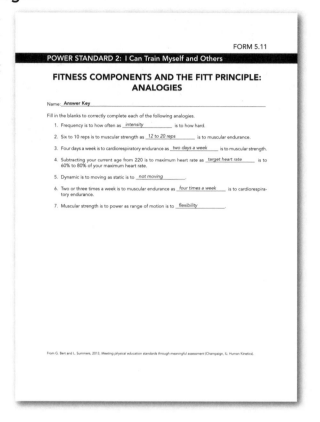

Benefits of Exercise 1: Concept Mapping

Students have been taught the physical, mental, and social benefits of exercise. This graphic organizer known as a concept map (form 5.12) can help students make connections to each of these concepts. To make the form more challenging, students can add more branches of concepts.

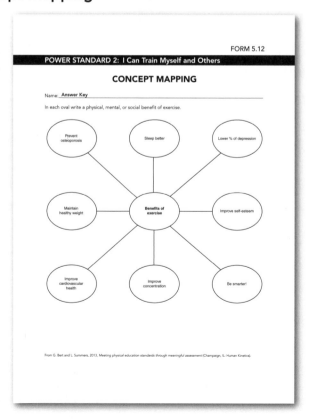

Benefits of Exercise 2: Graphic Organizer

Form 5.13 is a graphic organizer that challenges students to list the physical, mental, health-related, social, and aging benefits of exercise.

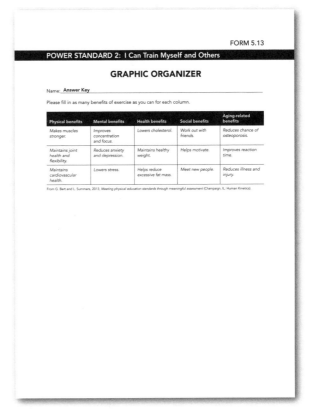

SPORT Principles 1: Concept Scaffolding

Students have been taught the SPORT training principles. In form 5.14, students explain what a SPORT training model is and then identify the correct answer from two choices for each of the principles.

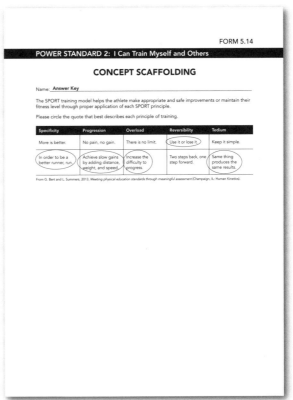

SPORT Principles 2: Story

Form 5.15 asks the student to apply each SPORT training principle by explaining how to become a better runner. The student needs to apply each principle of SPORT with regard to improving one's running.

SPORT Principles 3: Daily Scenario

Can students explain how we applied the SPORT training principles in class? Students can be challenged independently, collaborate in pairs or small groups, or review as an entire class. The idea is for students to realize how the SPORT training principles have been applied in various physical education activities. Form 5.15 is an example of answers you may get for a yoga class.

FITT Principle 1: Concept Scaffolding

Using the graphic organizer in form 5.16, students select the word that each letter of the FITT principle stands for.

After students can identify each letter of the FITT principle, they select what each letter means from four provided choices using the scaffolding method in form 5.17.

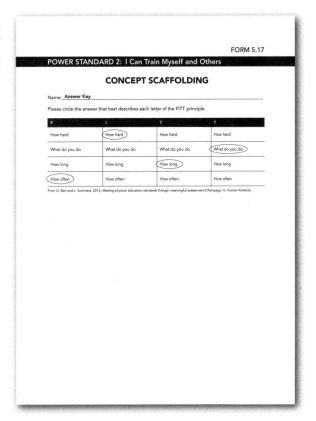

FITT Principle 2: Compare and Contrast

Using a Venn diagram in form 5.18, students write down the similarities and differences between two of the four FITT principles, intensity and type. This requires higher-level thinking and challenges students to list as many possible answers as they can.

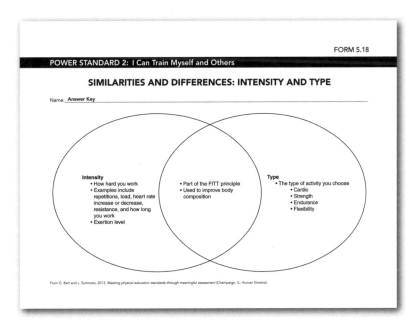

FITT and SPORT Principles: Checklists

Students have demonstrated understanding of the FITT and SPORT training principles. Form 5.19 lists training examples that students must match with one of three FITT training principles.

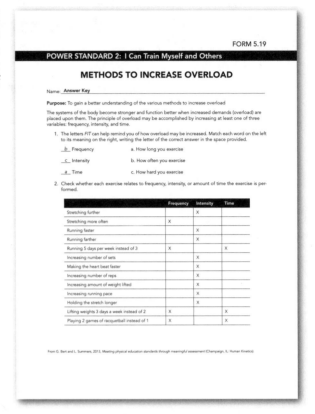

Students have been taught the concept of overload. Form 5.20 lists training examples that students must match with one of three types of overload.

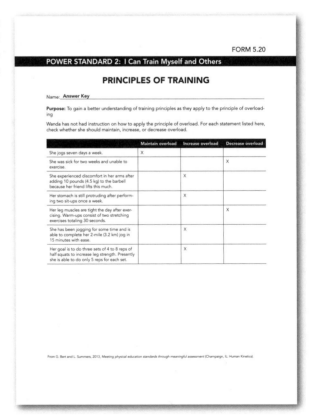

Exertion Levels: Pictures

Students analyze the pictures in form 5.21 and determine which pictures demonstrate an elevation of heart rate.

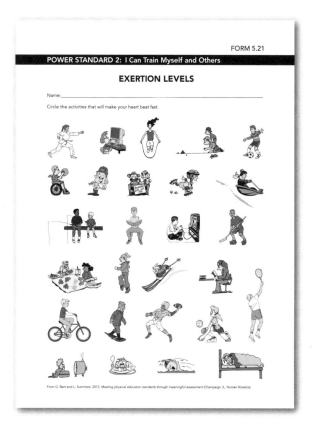

Summative Assessments

FITT Project

Students will choose one of three possible projects to demonstrate that they understand the FITT principle and fitness components (form 5.22). Forms 5.23 and 5.24 are examples of this summative assessment.

Form 5.23 is an example of a two-week fitness calendar that provides examples of the fitness components according to the FITT principle.

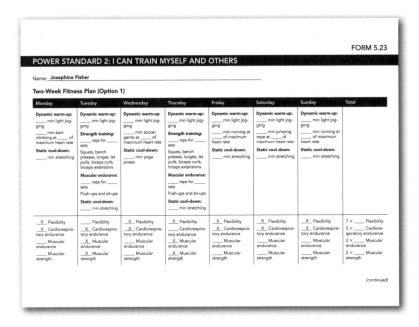

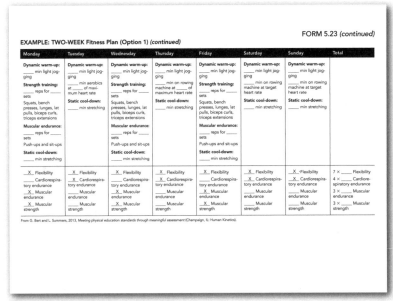

Form 5.24 is an example of how a student could use a graphic organizer to explain each of the fitness components according to the FITT principle.

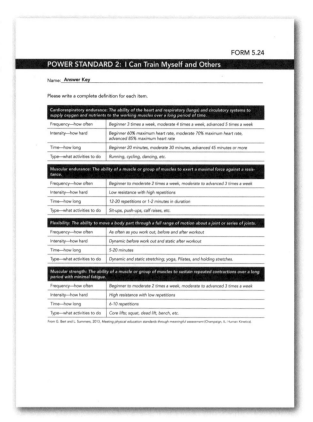

I Can Train Myself and Others: Self-Reflection

This self-reflective summative assessment asks students how they have demonstrated meeting or exceeding standard 2, "I can train myself and others" (form 5.25). Asking students to reflect on their own experiences and knowledge is a great way to assess application of this standard.

Posters

We post these information charts and visual aids on our walls, enlarging them to poster size. They illustrate the language and terminology we use when teaching these learning targets. We also provide these posters on our teacher webpage, which can help parents become familiar with the material taught in class and can be a great resource for students who miss class or need help.

This FITT principle and fitness components poster (form 5.26) is showcased in all of our teaching spaces.

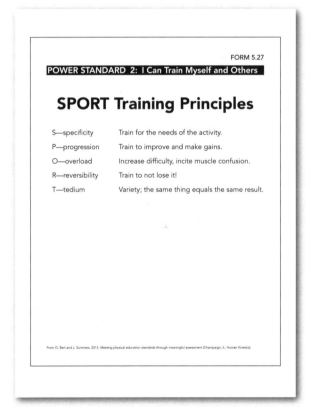

FORM 5.26

POWER STANDARD 2: I Can Train Myself and Others

FITT principle		Fitness level	Cardiorespiratory endurance	Muscular endurance	Muscular strength	Flexibility
Frequency	How often?	Beginner	3 days/wk	2 days/wk	2 days/wk	As often as you work out
		Moderate	4 days/wk	2 days/wk	2 days/wk	
		Athlete	5 days/wk	3 days/wk	3 days/wk	
Intensity	How hard?	Beginner	60% target heart rate	Low resistance High reps	High resistance Low reps	Dynamic before and static after
		Moderate	70% target heart rate			
		Athlete	85% target heart rate			
Time	How long?	Beginner	20 min	3-5 sets, 1-2 min each	3 sets, less than 1 min each	5-20 min
		Moderate	30 min			
		Athlete	45+ min			
Type	Which activities?	Beginner	Walk	Sit-ups	Core lifts	Dynamic and static
		Moderate	Jog			
		Athlete	Run			
Appropriate % of fat mass			Body composition			

From G. Bert and L. Summers, 2013, *Meeting physical education standards through meaningful assessment* (Champaign, IL: Human Kinetics).

This SPORT training poster (form 5.27) can help teach the principles and acts as a great visual aid.

FORM 5.27

POWER STANDARD 2: I Can Train Myself and Others

SPORT Training Principles

S—specificity	Train for the needs of the activity.
P—progression	Train to improve and make gains.
O—overload	Increase difficulty, incite muscle confusion.
R—reversibility	Train to not lose it!
T—tedium	Variety; the same thing equals the same result.

From G. Bert and L. Summers, 2013, *Meeting physical education standards through meaningful assessment* (Champaign, IL: Human Kinetics).

On form 5.28, we have explained the five fitness components. We make this into a poster that is used as a visual aid in all of our teaching spaces.

FORM 5.28

POWER STANDARD 2: I Can Train Myself and Others

Five Fitness Components of a Physically Educated Person

1. Cardiorespiratory endurance—The ability of the cardiovascular system (heart), respiratory system (lungs), and circulatory system to supply oxygen and nutrients to the working muscles over a long period of time.

2. Muscular strength—The ability of a muscle or group of muscles to exert a maximal force against a resistance.

3. Muscular endurance—The ability of a muscle or group of muscles to sustain repeated contractions over a long period of time with minimal fatigue.

4. Flexibility—The ability to move a body part through a full range of motion about a joint or a series of joints.

5. Body composition—The relative proportion of body fat to lean body mass.

From G. Bert and L. Summers, 2013, *Meeting physical education standards through meaningful assessment* (Champaign, IL: Human Kinetics).

CHAPTER 6

Power Standard 3: I Participate Regularly

In order to progress well in your studies, you must take at least two hours a day to exercise; for health must not be sacrificed to learning. . . . Walking is very important.

—Thomas Jefferson, from a letter to his nephew

Power standard: Student applies the FITT principle weekly. Student seeks activity and regularly participates in sport, games, and fitness.

KFO: I participate regularly.

Learning targets

- Students can locate and access opportunities for physical activity within the school setting.
- Students can locate and access opportunities for physical activity within the community.
- Students understand the similarities and differences between physical education and physical activity.
- Students can demonstrate participation in physical activity within the standards set by the CDC.
- Students understand the differences between lifetime fitness activities and lifetime sport activities.
- Students understand the three types of physical activities: aerobic, muscle strengthening, and bone strengthening (CDC, 2008).

From the CDC: www.cdc.gov/physicalactivity/everyone/guidelines/what_counts.html

ASSESSMENT FORMS

Formative Assessments

- Daily Pedometer Log (form 6.1)
- Activity Pyramid (form 6.2)
- Activity Checklist (form 6.3)

Summative Assessments

- Physical Activity Opportunities in My Community: Parks and Recreation (form 6.4)
- Physical Activity Opportunities in My Community: Fitness Industry (form 6.5)
- I Participate Regularly: Self-Reflection (form 6.6)

As physical educators, we need to extend experiences from in-class activity lessons to community and family activities. Simply put, we must prepare students for an active lifestyle away from the school setting. Eventually our students will leave school and move on to adulthood. We want our students to know how to exercise, where to go to exercise, and how to interact with the community in physical activity settings. High school physical educators need to remember that students might be taking their last physical education class. This could be their last opportunity to learn about the benefits of and the knowledge needed for participation in physical activity on a regular basis.

To promote exercise for its contribution to a healthy lifestyle, we need to develop assessments that encourage students to participate in physical activity for enjoyment, skill development, and health reasons. The learning targets for this chapter have been designed to teach students where to find opportunities for physical activity both outside of and within the school setting. All but one of the learning targets identify opportunities for activity outside of school because there are almost infinite opportunities beyond school and students will spend most of their lives outside the confines of physical education class.

The formative assessments in this chapter equip students with the knowledge of how to use pedometers in order to assess physical activity. We want students to know that taking at least 10,000 steps each day will improve their overall health and wellness. Using pedometers in a variety of physical activity settings will give students the idea that physical activity comes in many styles and intensity levels. With these assessments, students are tracking physical activity with pedometers and at the same time trying a variety of activities that they may not have done before.

The summative assessments in the chapter challenge students to go out into the community and participate in activity in either a park and recreation or fitness industry setting. Both are valid options that will be available to secondary students after high school, and the assessments are important in order to prepare students for these two types of activity settings.

We have developed the following assessments so that students can successfully demonstrate, "I participate regularly!"

Formative Assessments

With these assessments, students track what exercise looks like in their personal lives: fitness components involved, how often, how hard, duration, and type of activities. What we like most about these assessments is how easy they are to use—students can use them all year long and can share them with friends and family members. Students get a great idea of how active and inactive they are while inside and outside of class.

Daily Pedometer Log

Form 6.1 is a template for recording total steps taken per day for seven days using a pedometer. Students wear pedometers all day and record their total steps each day. The goal is 10,000 to 12,000 steps each day.

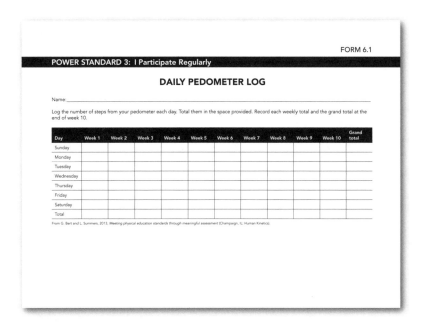

Activity Pyramid

The template in form 6.2 is an excellent method for assessing the activity of secondary students as well as elementary students. In each section, students write the activities performed that day, indicating the date, time, and activity involved. This is an excellent homework assignment. Be prepared to provide multiple copies to students—many students will want to record this information more than once or twice a week!

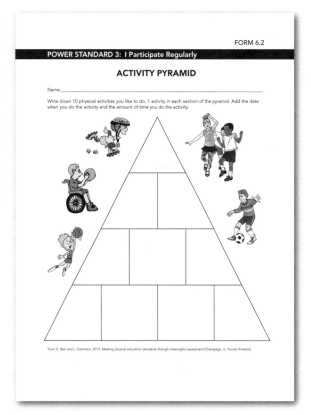

Activity Checklist

Form 6.3 is a monthly activity tracker for use by upper-elementary to secondary students. The goal is to perform two to three activities for 20 minutes at a time for a total of 60 minutes per day. Or, this form may be used to track participation on a monthly basis.

FORM 6.3

POWER STANDARD 3: I Participate Regularly

ACTIVITY CHECKLIST

Name: __Arthur Finn__

Place a mark next to each of the activities you participate in for at least 20 minutes this month.

X	Running	X	Walking a dog
	Jumping rope		Swimming laps
	Shooting hoops	X	Jogging on a treadmill
	Stair-climbing		Rowing
	Aerobics	X	Swing dancing
	Kickboxing		Pilates
	Yoga		Taking a hike
X	Geocaching	X	Playing soccer
X	Tennis		Badminton
	Football		Tai chi
	Chopping wood		Pickleball
	Golf		Fishing
	Lacrosse		Field hockey
	Rugby		Roller-skating
	Bike riding		Skateboarding
	Wakeboarding		Downhill skiing
	Waterskiing		Snowboarding
	Snowshoeing		Cross-country skiing
	Wii Fit	X	Dance Dance Revolution
	Elliptical		Health club class
	Raking leaves	X	Stretching
X	Weight training	X	Core ball
	Resistance bands		Scuba diving
X	Horseback riding		Kayaking
X	Rock climbing		Surfing

From G. Bert and L. Summers, 2013, *Meeting physical education standards through meaningful assessment* (Champaign, IL: Human Kinetics).

Summative Assessments

With these summative assessments, we are providing an opportunity for students to explore the fitness and sport opportunities available within the community, and we ask them to provide a written self-reflection. The Greek philosopher Socrates once said, "The unexamined life is not worth living." We ask students to reflect on their weaknesses, strengths, and habits with regard to regular participation in physical activity. Honest self-reflection is challenging but crucial.

Physical Activity Opportunities in My Community: Parks and Recreation

The summative assessment in form 6.4 asks students to either write an essay or provide photos or illustrations indicating how to access parks and recreation activities in their community.

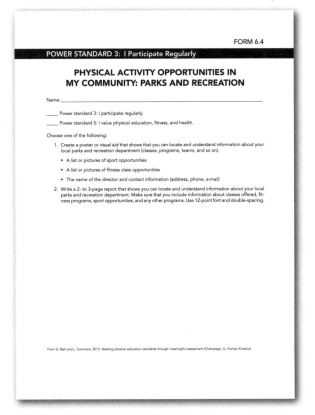

Physical Activity Opportunities in My Community: Fitness Industry

Form 6.5 is a summative assessment that asks students to access their local fitness establishments. Students may create a visual aid or write an essay explaining various programs offered at their local fitness clubs. This is a valuable assessment for high school students who are ready to graduate.

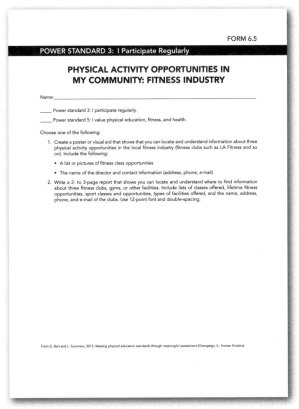

I Participate Regularly: Self-Reflection

Form 6.6 is our end-of-term summative assessment that directs students to write an essay. Students are asked to recall, form opinions, and communicate how they meet this standard. They are asked to provide examples and argue their points of view.

FORM 6.6

POWER STANDARD 3: I Participate Regularly

SELF-REFLECTION

Name:_____

_____ Student applies the FITT principle weekly. Student seeks activity and regularly participates in sport, games, and fitness.

Please explain how you meet or exceed this standard. In your answer, include how you demonstrate your level of participation in class and outside of class as it pertains to the application of the FITT principle and daily activity recommendations. Because you are proving to the reader that you meet or exceed this standard, it is critical to use many examples, both general and specific. What does participation in fitness, sport, and games look like for you each day, week, and month?

From G. Bert and L. Summers, 2013, *Meeting physical education standards through meaningful assessment* (Champaign, IL: Human Kinetics).

CHAPTER 7

Power Standard 4: I Am Fit

No matter who you are, no matter what you do, you absolutely, positively do have the power to change.

—Bill Phillips

Power standard: Student acquires the knowledge of skills necessary to maintain a health-enhancing level of physical fitness.

KFO: I am fit.

Learning targets

- Students can achieve targeted levels of fitness as measured through fitness testing and assessments (e.g., Fitnessgram, President's Challenge, state, district, and school fitness testing).
- Students understand and analyze personal areas of strengths and weaknesses and apply training principles to maintain or improve scores to healthy fitness zones.

ASSESSMENT FORMS

Formative and Summative Assessments

- I Am Fit Versus I Am Not Fit (form 7.1)
- Fitness Tracker (form 7.2)
- Fitness Log (form 7.3)
- Fitness Profile (form 7.4)
- I Am Fit: Self-Reflection (form 7.5)

Posters

- Fitness Goals (form 7.6)

A major challenge for physical educators is accurately assessing students' fitness. We ask ourselves: How can we assess fitness fairly and appropriately? How can we prepare our students to maintain and sustain fitness? How can we formulate assessments that encourage students to improve and aspire to demonstrate fitness? We have learned that our students assume greater self-responsibility in their lives and display greater autonomy with regard to their personal fitness behaviors than we might assume. They are largely independent in assessing their personal fitness and health status. They can interpret information from fitness tests and use this information to plan and design their own programs to achieve and maintain personal fitness goals that encompass all fitness components. Our students demonstrate that they are able to monitor and adjust a personal fitness program to meet their needs and goals to maintain appropriate levels of cardiorespiratory endurance, muscular strength and endurance, flexibility, and body composition. In this chapter, we share six assessments that will help students to proudly declare, "I am fit!"

Formative and Summative Assessments

Because fitness does not happen overnight, our assessments rely on properly training students in our classes. Our assessments can be both a method to check the progress of students' fitness as well as a final summation of their fitness goals, tests, and personal journey. So for this standard, formative and summative assessments are not considered separately the way they are for the other standards.

Form 7.1 is a T-chart assignment that directs students to list and synthesize information about the characteristics of the body, or being physically fit versus physically unfit. Students are free to select any criteria of physical fitness, such as body type, overall health, exertion levels, activity levels, fitness measurements, body composition, diseases, and many others.

FORM 7.1

POWER STANDARD 4: I Am Fit

I AM FIT VERSUS I AM NOT FIT

Name: **Answer Key**

Compare the differences between being fit and being unfit on the following T-chart.

I am fit.	I am not fit.
Passes health-related fitness tests.	Does not pass health-related fitness tests or only passes a few.
Has healthy body composition.	Body-fat percentage is higher than 25%.
Demonstrates muscular endurance, muscular strength, cardiorespiratory endurance, and flexibility.	Does not demonstrate muscular endurance, muscular strength, cardiorespiratory endurance, or flexibility.
Has healthy blood pressure and heart rate (120/80).	Has high blood pressure.
	Easily winded and tired.

From G. Bert and L. Summers, 2013, *Meeting physical education standards through meaningful assessment* (Champaign, IL: Human Kinetics).

Form 7.2 is a recording sheet for fitness goals, baseline fitness measurements, and future physical fitness test scores, including three sequential posttest scores after baseline measurements. Each of the fitness components is tested and assessed. Students write their goals in the space provided at the bottom of this form.

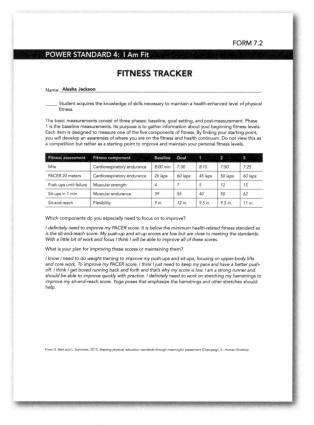

Form 7.3 requires students to log and record their fitness activities. This is a 12-week assignment. Students perform three cardio, strength, and flexibility workouts each week for 12 weeks. This can be done in school, out of school, or a combination of both. We have used this form for both formative and summative assessments.

Form 7.4 allows students to record their fitness profile. Part I is a recording sheet for body measurements using skin calipers.

Part II asks students to reflect on family history of diseases associated with a sedentary lifestyle, and part III asks students to reflect upon their exercise lifestyle. This is an excellent summative assessment.

We use form 7.5 as an end-of-term summative assessment. Students are putting all of the assessments in this chapter together and reflecting on their overall health and wellness in regard to physical fitness. Students must explain and argue their points as to how they either met or did not meet this standard.

Poster

Form 7.6 is a poster that teachers can easily adapt to post on the walls of teaching stations. It lists fitness goals for both boys and girls. Our school district uses the following fitness tests each year for all grade levels: sit-and-reach, 20-meter PACER test, mile run, sit-ups to failure (meaning go until you can no longer perform), and push-ups to failure. Our students do well on these tests and many meet the healthy fitness zones. Because our students needed to be challenged more, we collectively agreed to create our own fitness standards, and we developed four levels of fitness. Because our mascot is the wolf, our progressing levels from fit to fittest are pup, yearling, wolf, and leader of the pack.

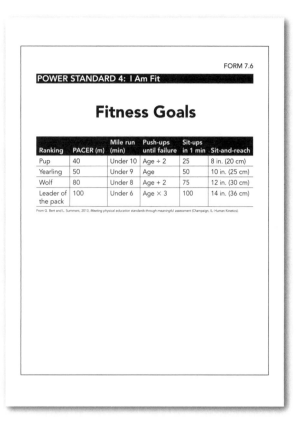

FORM 7.6

POWER STANDARD 4: I Am Fit

Fitness Goals

Ranking	PACER (m)	Mile run (min)	Push-ups until failure	Sit-ups in 1 min	Sit-and-reach
Pup	40	Under 10	Age ÷ 2	25	8 in. (20 cm)
Yearling	50	Under 9	Age	50	10 in. (25 cm)
Wolf	80	Under 8	Age + 2	75	12 in. (30 cm)
Leader of the pack	100	Under 6	Age × 3	100	14 in. (36 cm)

From G. Bert and L. Summers, 2013, *Meeting physical education standards through meaningful assessment* (Champaign, IL: Human Kinetics).

CHAPTER 8

Power Standard 5: I Can Play Fairly

Excellence is not a singular act but a habit. You are what you do repeatedly.

—Shaquille O'Neal

Power standard: Student exhibits responsible personal and social behavior that respects self and others in physical activity settings.

KFO: I can play fairly.

Learning targets

- Students apply SOTG in fitness activities, sport, and games.
- Students are able to self-officiate.
- Students demonstrate positive communication: praise, motivation, and encouragement.
- Students demonstrate and sustain positive, active participation.

ASSESSMENT FORMS

Formative Assessments

- Active Participation: Concept Scaffolding (forms 8.1-8.3)
- I Can Play Fairly Checklists (forms 8.4-8.5)
- Spirit of the Game Short Response (form 8.6)

Summative Assessments

- Spirit of the Game Project (form 8.7)
- I Can Play Fairly: Self-Reflection (form 8.8)

Posters

- Spirit of the Game (form 8.9)
- Ten Things You Should Know About Spirit of the Game (form 8.10)

With power standard 5, we are assessing self-initiated behaviors that promote personal and group success in activity settings. These include safe practices, adherence to rules, self-officiating, etiquette, cooperation and teamwork, ethical behavior, positive social interaction, and participation. All of the learning targets help teach students the levels of the Pyramid of Active Participation. Our goal is to assess and record our students achieving each level of the pyramid. The entire purpose of this standard is to teach students about appropriate behavior in sport and games. Appropriate behavior makes sport and games fun for everyone during participation. When students can enjoy sport and games, they achieve more success in the activities and are more likely to participate in them because everyone is helping to make the game fun for each other.

Assessing behavior can be challenging. The word *behavior* can imply subjectivity, but we have attempted to keep the assessment of this standard objective. With emphasis placed on SOTG (spirit of the game) and the Pyramid of Active Participation, these assessments encourage students to show that they can play fairly. The Pyramid of Active Participation is based on four levels of self-initiated behaviors. The most bottom level is moving without a ball, such as V-pattern cutting, L-pattern cutting, and perhaps just concentrating on moving! When students perform these

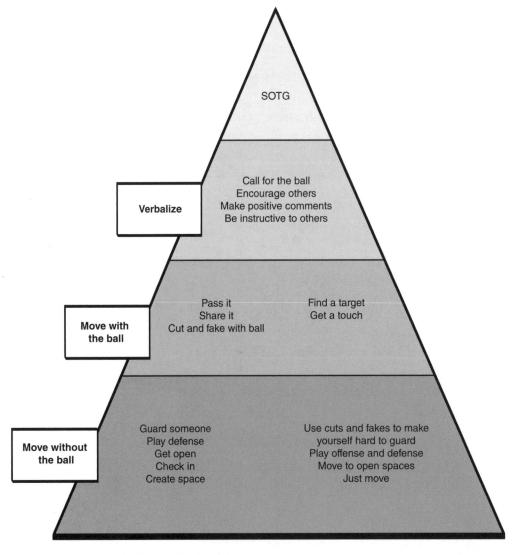

FIGURE 8.1 Pyramid of Active Participation.

basic off-ball movements, the game is more enjoyable for both offensive and defensive players—everyone is participating with purpose or intent. The second level of the pyramid involves students moving with a ball, such as passing, dribbling, sharing, looking for receivers, and involving others by being productive teammates. The third level involves verbalizing language that is helpful, instructive, and welcoming to others. The fourth level is the leadership level, which challenges students to teach others and to use their advanced skills in order to help others or assist the teacher. The top level of the pyramid is SOTG—when students demonstrate mastery of the four lower levels, they possess SOTG!

Formative Assessments

The formative assessments focus on active participation and SOTG in activity settings. They involve teacher, self-, and peer observations.

Active Participation: Concept Scaffolding

On form 8.1, students recall various movements they can perform without the ball in sport and games. We are looking for students to distinguish what constitutes as moving without a ball in a gamelike setting. Many educators assume that students know what to do with and without the ball; however, we do need to teach these concepts and assess them. The answers serve only as examples; there are many other examples of moving without the ball.

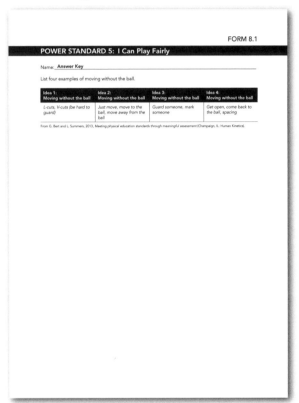

FORM 8.1

POWER STANDARD 5: I Can Play Fairly

Name: **Answer Key**

List four examples of moving without the ball.

Idea 1: Moving without the ball	Idea 2: Moving without the ball	Idea 3: Moving without the ball	Idea 4: Moving without the ball
L-cuts, V-cuts (be hard to guard)	Just move, move to the ball, move away from the ball	Guard someone, mark someone	Get open, come back to the ball, spacing

From G. Bart and L. Summers, 2013, Meeting physical education standards through meaningful assessment (Champaign, IL: Human Kinetics).

Form 8.2 is similar to form 8.1. In this case, students give examples of what to do with the ball in sport and games. There are more possibilities that can fit this assessment; we offer here just a few examples.

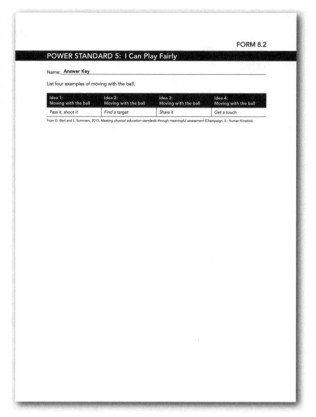

On form 8.3, students are asked to recall four possibilities of verbal communication during sport and games. Our goal is to help students know what to say when they participate in physical activities. We have listed examples of encouragement, compliments, calling for the ball, and instructional comments.

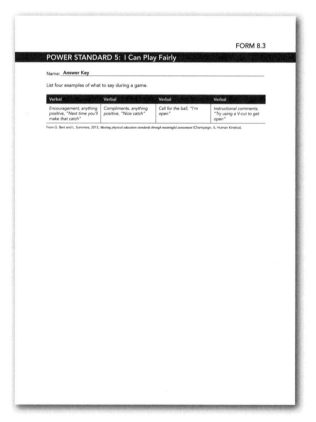

I Can Play Fairly Checklists

Working in pairs, students use form 8.4 to report what they observed both of their partner and themselves with regard to moving without the ball.

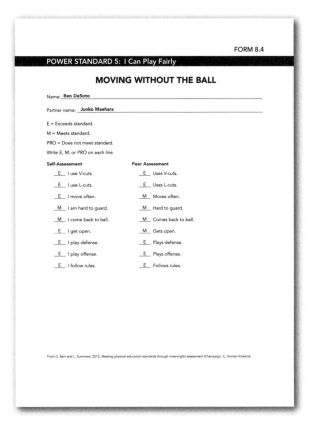

Similar to the previous assignment, on form 8.5 students report what they observed of their partner and themselves with regard to moving with the ball and listening for positive verbal comments.

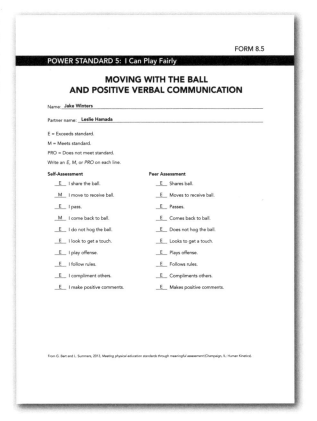

Short Response

Students use self-reflection to share how their behavior looks. Using form 8.6, students write about their strengths in meeting this standard.

Summative Assessments

Form 8.7 is a summative assessment with three options. The first option directs students to make a poster, visual aid, or collage that illustrates what it means to play fair and show respect for the game and others. Students also have the option to write an essay or discuss the characteristics of fair play and respect for the game.

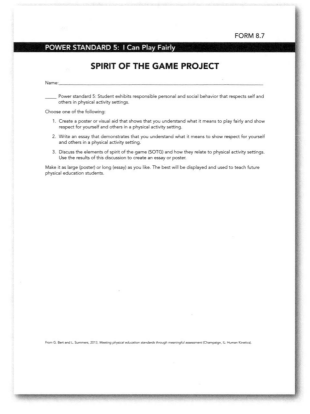

Form 8.8 is a summative assessment in the form of an end-of-term essay. It requires that students compose and argue their point of view in writing as to how they meet power standard 5, "I can play fairly." Students are self-reflective in essay form as they discuss how they displayed SOTG and how they were active participants.

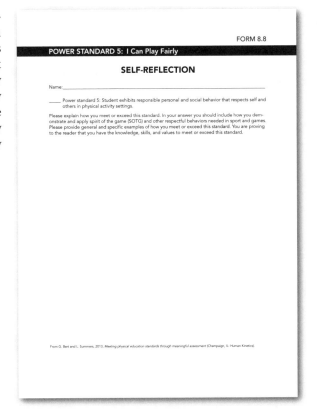

Posters

We post both of these posters on our walls and refer to them if students need clarification on SOTG. It reminds our students what physical education should look like, what it should sound like, and what each participant's experience can be.

Form 8.9 is a template for a poster that can be displayed in teaching stations. It defines SOTG.

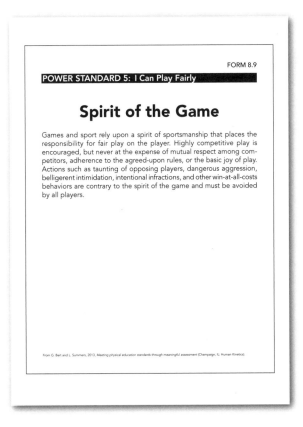

Form 8.10 is another template for a poster that can be displayed. It shares 10 things you should know about SOTG.

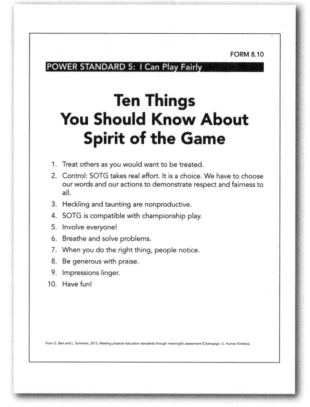

FORM 8.10

POWER STANDARD 5: I Can Play Fairly

Ten Things You Should Know About Spirit of the Game

1. Treat others as you would want to be treated.
2. Control: SOTG takes real effort. It is a choice. We have to choose our words and our actions to demonstrate respect and fairness to all.
3. Heckling and taunting are nonproductive.
4. SOTG is compatible with championship play.
5. Involve everyone!
6. Breathe and solve problems.
7. When you do the right thing, people notice.
8. Be generous with praise.
9. Impressions linger.
10. Have fun!

From G. Bert and L. Summers, 2013, *Meeting physical education standards through meaningful assessment* (Champaign, IL: Human Kinetics).

CHAPTER 9

Power Standard 6: I Value Physical Education, Fitness, and Health

Every human being is the author of his own health or disease.

—Buddha

Power standard: Student chooses to live a healthy and fit life.

KFO: I value physical education, fitness, and health.

Learning targets

- Students are able to find fitness and related activities in their community and other communities.
- Students motivate themselves and others toward fitness.
- Students value setting goals and monitoring fitness progress and maintenance.
- Students actively engage in exercise, sport, and fitness.

ASSESSMENT FORMS

Formative Assessments

- Campus Recreation Research Project (form 9.1)
- Local Fitness Options Research Project (form 9.2)
- Yoga or Pilates Prescription (forms 9.3-9.5)
- Sign Up for an Event (form 9.6)
- Learn by Teaching: Yoga (form 9.7)
- Active Participation Scaffolding (forms 9.8-9.11)
- Active Participation Checklists (forms 9.12-9.14)

Summative Assessments

- Personal Fitness Profile and Self-Reflection: Compare and Contrast Fitness Profiles (form 9.15)
- SMART Fitness Goals: Cardiorespiratory Endurance (form 9.16)
- SMART Fitness Goals: Muscular Endurance (form 9.17)
- SMART Fitness Goals: Flexibility (form 9.18)
- Fitness Calendar (form 9.19)
- Personal Fitness and Nutrition Log (form 9.20)
- I Value Physical Education, Fitness, and Health: Self-Reflection (form 9.21)

As physical education teachers, we want to help students understand that physical activity is an important part of everyday living and to help them experience the satisfaction and joy that result from learning about and participating in physical activity regularly. The intent of power standard 6 is for students to develop an awareness of the intrinsic values and benefits of participation in physical activities that provide personal meaning. As a result of these intrinsic benefits of participation, students learn to pursue lifelong physical activities that meet their needs.

The assessments for this particular chapter include goal setting, logs, journaling, teaching others, and locating and accessing physical activity opportunities in the community. A major goal of this standard is to give students the tools and knowledge to seek out fitness within their community. For years we assumed our students knew how to locate and access health clubs, sport programs (adult leagues, city parks and recreation leagues), outdoor fitness opportunities such as running events and community walking trails, golf courses, swimming pools, and other fitness-related leisure activities. What we found, however, was that students did not know how to access and locate these opportunities, so we decided to include this in our curriculum. Another goal of this standard is to create an environment where students value motivating themselves and others while engaged in physical activities. We do this by teaching SMART goal setting, logging and reporting physical activity, and giving positive feedback via our Pyramid of Active Participation.

Formative Assessments

We divide assessment of this standard into five areas:

1. **Projects.** We assign projects that are done at home. The projects are designed to get students out into the community researching what fitness and sport activities are available to them after school, on weekends, and into adulthood. High school students need to tap into the fitness industry, local parks and recreation, and city leagues and explore their options. Projects are assessed according to the criteria and completeness of the grading rubric with each assignment. They may also be assessed for completeness only; this is how we assess our fitness calendar assignment.

2. **Online assignments.** Online assignments enable students to gain knowledge pertaining to various online fitness calculators. Students can then self-assess and reflect upon their fitness status. The Internet is full of calculators for all fitness components. This process directs students where to go online to do fitness calculations and assess their personal fitness levels.

3. **Self-reflection.** Self-reflection allows students to further explore personal fitness needs, scores, and physical activity options. Through self-reflection, students can explore personal strengths and weaknesses. We use fitness diaries, fitness logs, short-answer and open-ended questioning, and other strategies to achieve this. Self-reflection is a type of questioning where students are required to critique and analyze information presented to them. Analyzing information through questioning is a research-based technique used in many education settings (Marzano, 2001).

4. **Teacher assessment of active, in-class participation.** This is a difficult area to assess because measuring effort levels can be subjective, which is not what we want in an assessment. But there are areas of effort and certain behaviors that teachers and students can track so that students receive a snapshot of what they look like while participating. We call this *active participation*, and we use checklists and charts to assess it. Active participation checklists track behaviors such as running, passing, sharing the ball, moving without the ball, stepping to the ball, and other game-like behavior. Active participation behaviors are common in many lifetime, recreational, intramural, and team sports that students may choose to participate in. We believe

that with a little skill proficiency and knowing how to be active, students will become successful participants in lifetime activities (see chapter 1).

5. **Direct observation of students.** We mentioned the Pyramid of Active Participation in chapters 2 and 8. The four levels that we teach to our students are SOTG (spirit of the game), what to say during participation, what to do with the ball, and what to do without the ball. Our pyramid template is shown in figure 8.1.

Campus Recreation Research Project

Our objective with this project (form 9.1) is to get students researching what a college or university offers for intramurals, club sport, fitness, and related employment opportunities. The purpose is to connect sport, games, and fitness with university life.

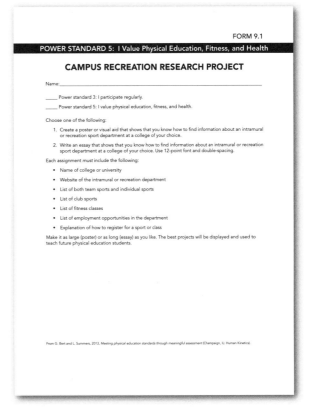

Local Fitness Options Research Project

Form 9.2 is a template for an assignment that gets students out in the community researching their local parks and recreation department and exploring its opportunities for activity.

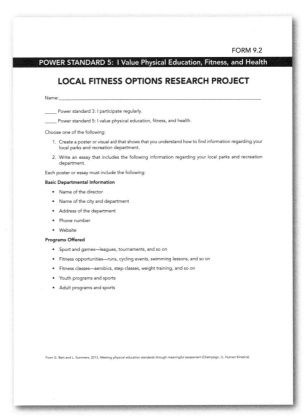

Yoga or Pilates Prescription

In this project (forms 9.3-9.5), students choose medical conditions and make a one- to two-page handout describing how yoga or Pilates can alleviate the symptoms of the ailment. We want students to be able to identify which poses can help prevent, rehabilitate, and aid healing of a variety of common physical and emotional conditions. All of the assignments are collected by the teacher and made into a book at the end of the term.

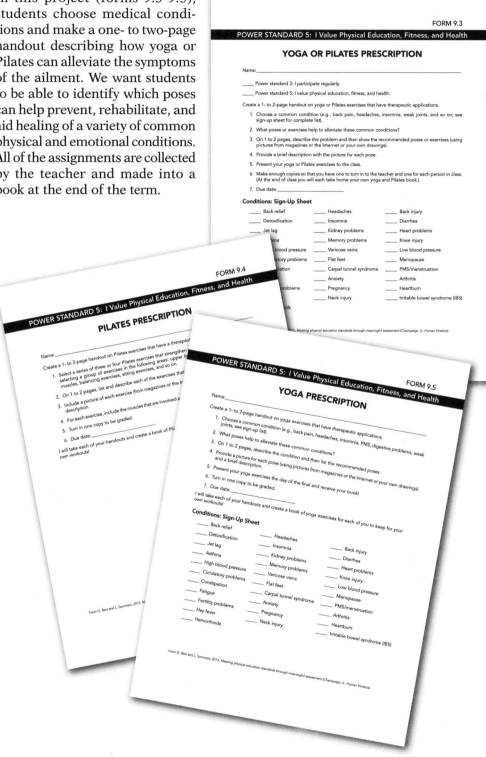

FORM 9.3

POWER STANDARD 5: I Value Physical Education, Fitness, and Health

YOGA OR PILATES PRESCRIPTION

Name:_____

_____ Power standard 3: I participate regularly.

_____ Power standard 5: I value physical education, fitness, and health.

Create a 1- to 2-page handout on yoga or Pilates exercises that have therapeutic applications.

1. Choose a common condition (e.g., back pain, headaches, insomnia, weak joints, and so on; see sign-up sheet for complete list).

2. What poses or exercises help to alleviate these common conditions?

3. On 1 to 2 pages, describe the problem and then show the recommended poses or exercises (using pictures from magazines or the Internet or your own drawings).

4. Provide a brief description with the picture for each pose.

5. Present your yoga or Pilates exercises to the class.

6. Make enough copies so that you have one to turn in to the teacher and one for each person in class. (At the end of class you will each take home your own yoga and Pilates book.)

7. Due date:_____

Conditions: Sign-Up Sheet

_____ Back relief	_____ Headaches	_____ Back injury
_____ Detoxification	_____ Insomnia	_____ Diarrhea
_____ Jet lag	_____ Kidney problems	_____ Heart problems
_____ ...ma	_____ Memory problems	_____ Knee injury
_____ ...blood pressure	_____ Varicose veins	_____ Low blood pressure
_____ ...tory problems	_____ Flat feet	_____ Menopause
_____ ...ation	_____ Carpal tunnel syndrome	_____ PMS/menstruation
	_____ Anxiety	_____ Arthritis
_____ ...roblems	_____ Pregnancy	_____ Heartburn
	_____ Neck injury	_____ Irritable bowel syndrome (IBS)
_____ ...ds		

...3, Meeting physical education standards through meaningful assessment (Champaign, IL: Human Kinetics).

FORM 9.4

POWER STANDARD 5: I Value Physical Education, Fitness, and Health

PILATES PRESCRIPTION

Name:_____

Create a 1- to 2-page handout on Pilates exercises that have a therapeu...

1. Select a series of three or four Pilates exercises that strengthen... selecting a group of exercises in the following areas: upper b... muscles, balancing exercises, sitting exercises, and so on.

2. On 1 to 2 pages, list and describe each of the exercises that...

3. Include a picture of each exercise (from magazines or the In... description.

4. For each exercise, include the muscles that are involved a...

5. Turn in one copy to be graded.

6. Due date:_____

I will take each of your handouts and create a book of Pila... own workouts!

From G. Bert and L. Summers, 2013, M...

FORM 9.5

POWER STANDARD 5: I Value Physical Education, Fitness, and Health

YOGA PRESCRIPTION

Name:_____

Create a 1- to 2-page handout on yoga exercises that have therapeutic applications.

1. Choose a common condition (e.g., back pain, headaches, insomnia, PMS, digestive problems, weak joints; see sign-up list).

2. What poses help to alleviate these common conditions?

3. On 1 to 2 pages, describe the condition and then list the recommended poses.

4. Provide a picture for each pose (using pictures from magazines or the Internet or your own drawings) and a brief description.

5. Present your yoga exercises the day of the final and receive your book!

6. Turn in one copy to be graded.

7. Due date:_____

I will take each of your handouts and create a book of yoga exercises for each of you to keep for your own workouts!

Conditions: Sign-Up Sheet

_____ Back relief		
_____ Detoxification	_____ Headaches	
_____ Jet lag	_____ Insomnia	_____ Back injury
_____ Asthma	_____ Kidney problems	_____ Diarrhea
_____ High blood pressure	_____ Memory problems	_____ Heart problems
_____ Circulatory problems	_____ Varicose veins	_____ Knee injury
_____ Constipation	_____ Flat feet	_____ Low blood pressure
_____ Fatigue	_____ Carpal tunnel syndrome	_____ Menopause
_____ Fertility problems	_____ Anxiety	_____ PMS/menstruation
_____ Hay fever	_____ Pregnancy	_____ Arthritis
_____ Hemorrhoids	_____ Neck injury	_____ Heartburn
		_____ Irritable bowel syndrome (IBS)

From G. Bert and L. Summers, 2013, Meeting physical education standards through meaningful assessment (Champaign, IL: Human Kinetics).

We have provided a list of conditions on form 9.3. Students sign up and choose a condition so that there are no duplicates. This is just our list; teachers are free to select others if applicable.

Back relief	Headaches	Back injury
Detoxification	Insomnia	Diarrhea
Jet lag	Kidney problems	Heart problems
Asthma	Memory problems	Knee injury
High blood pressure	Varicose veins	Low blood pressure
Circulatory problems	Flat feet	Menopause
Constipation	Carpal tunnel syndrome	PMS/menstruation
Fatigue	Anxiety	Arthritis
Fertility problems	Pregnancy	Heartburn
Hay fever	Neck injury	Irritable bowel syndrome (IBS)
Hemorrhoids		

Sign Up for an Event

One of our goals is to teach students how to participate in community fitness events. In this assignment (form 9.6), students make a poster or visual aid showing that they know how to find and sign up for fitness events (e.g., runs, cycling, triathlons, swim meets). We often assume that students know how to access fitness outside of school, but do they know how to sign up for a race? Do they know what to do at the event? This assignment helps them to learn these skills: finding an event, registering for an event, and knowing what to do at the event.

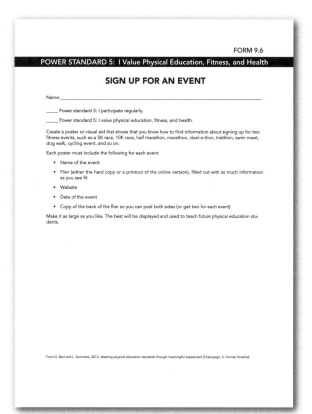

FORM 9.6

POWER STANDARD 5: I Value Physical Education, Fitness, and Health

SIGN UP FOR AN EVENT

Name:_____

_____ Power standard 3: I participate regularly.

_____ Power standard 5: I value physical education, fitness, and health.

Create a poster or visual aid that shows that you know how to find information about signing up for two fitness events, such as a 5K race, 10K race, half marathon, marathon, duel-a-thon, triathlon, swim meet, dog walk, cycling event, and so on.

Each poster must include the following for each event:

- Name of the event
- Flier (either the hard copy or a printout of the online version), filled out with as much information as you see fit
- Website
- Date of the event
- Copy of the back of the flier so you can post both sides (or get two for each event)

Make it as large as you like. The best will be displayed and used to teach future physical education students.

From G. Bert and L. Summers, 2013, *Meeting physical education standards through meaningful assessment* (Champaign, IL: Human Kinetics).

Learn by Teaching

According to Bloom's taxonomy, the highest level of learning occurs when we teach others. This assignment challenges students to teach the sun salutation to someone else. Using form 9.7, students teach the sun salutation to a parent, guardian, or friend at home and answer questions about their teaching.

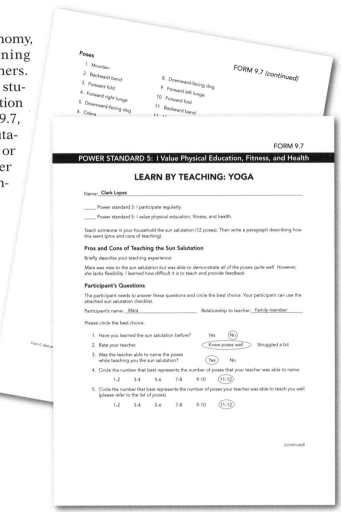

Teacher Assessment of Active Participation

We use a rubric for active participation in physical education. We all have been challenged with students who behave well, dress down, show up on a regular basis, and yet do not do anything. This student tends to be the sedentary, nondefiant type who probably just needs a clearer definition of what it means to be active. After all, active participation in physical education class is a sign of respect for others and oneself. Inactive people take the fun away from the activity for themselves and others.

Our rubric is similar to the Hellison model of teaching responsibility through physical activity (Hellison, 2011). The Hellison model consists of five levels of responsibility and corresponds nicely with power standard 5: Student exhibits responsible personal and social behavior that respects self and others in physical activity settings. The five levels of responsibility in the Hellison model are irresponsibility (level 1), self-control (level 2), involvement (level 3), self-responsibility (level 4), and caring (level 5). This is a helpful model for teaching personal behavior skills in any activity setting. We have tried to enhance this model by associating with each level specific movement behaviors that reflect power standard 5.

We will begin by including our scaffolding templates for our active participation model.

Active Participation Scaffolding

In this assessment (form 9.8), students choose two traits from examples provided from the Pyramid of Active Participation.

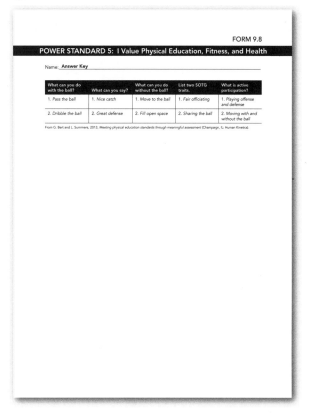

The assessment in form 9.9 directs students to list seven possibilities of moving without the ball.

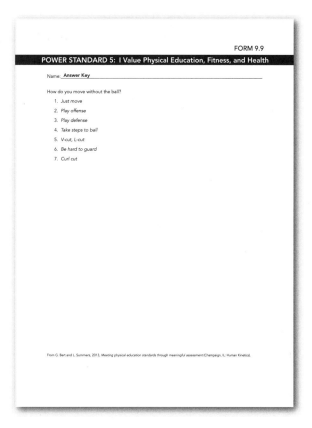

The assessment in form 9.10 directs students to list five possibilities of moving with the ball.

The assessment in form 9.11 directs students to list what to say and listen for during activity.

Active Participation Checklists

This assignment asks students to assess their teammates on particular levels of the Pyramid of Active Participation: moving without the ball, moving with the ball, and verbalizing. This helps students distinguish what constitutes being active. The first assessment, form 9.12, is about movement without the ball.

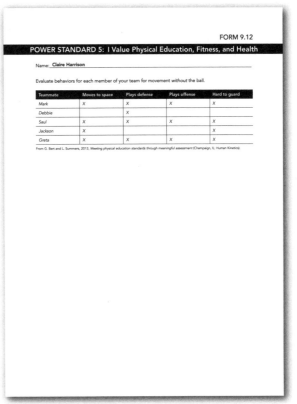

FORM 9.12

POWER STANDARD 5: I Value Physical Education, Fitness, and Health

Name: __Claire Harrison__

Evaluate behaviors for each member of your team for movement without the ball.

Teammate	Moves to space	Plays defense	Plays offense	Hard to guard
Mark	X	X	X	X
Debbie		X		
Saul	X	X	X	X
Jackson	X			X
Greta	X	X	X	X

From G. Bert and L. Summers, 2013, Meeting physical education standards through meaningful assessment (Champaign, IL: Human Kinetics).

With form 9.13, students are evaluating behaviors of teammates for movement with the ball.

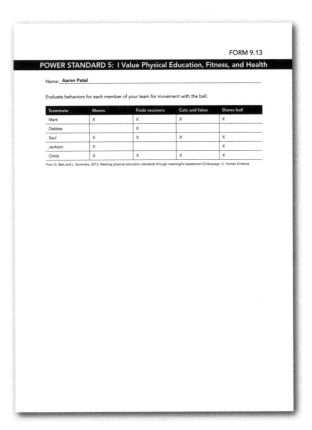

FORM 9.13

POWER STANDARD 5: I Value Physical Education, Fitness, and Health

Name: __Aaron Patel__

Evaluate behaviors for each member of your team for movement with the ball.

Teammate	Moves	Finds receivers	Cuts and fakes	Shares ball
Mark	X	X	X	X
Debbie		X		
Saul	X	X	X	X
Jackson	X			X
Greta	X	X	X	X

From G. Bert and L. Summers, 2013, Meeting physical education standards through meaningful assessment (Champaign, IL: Human Kinetics).

Students use form 9.14 to evaluate behaviors of teammates regarding what to say and what to listen for during games.

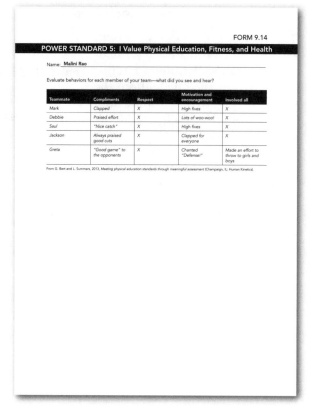

Summative Assessments

Sponsoring Your Own School Run

One way to promote physical activity that has been successful at Black Hills High School involves organizing a school run. We do this annually around Memorial Day. Staff, students, teachers, and parents are all invited and encouraged to attend. Our physical education teachers serve as course marshals, starters, and supporters and make sure enough first aid and water are available. Students can receive extra credit for participating, but more importantly, they learn what is involved with entering a community run. We hope this run, along with our Sign Up for an Event assignment, will teach and encourage students to become involved in community fitness events (e.g., runs, triathlons, cycling and walking events).

To add a little spice to this event, we order race numbers with our school colors and logo. Each student receives a race number bib and keeps it as a memento.

Personal Fitness Profile and Self-Reflection

Physical fitness is a personal matter. Our job is to teach students the skills to self-assess and train for healthy fitness levels as reflected on fitness tests, such as Fitnessgram. Everyone grows and matures at different rates, and therefore we do not assign grades for physical fitness scores. We do assess knowledge of the fitness concepts and SPORT training principles and how they apply to the FITT principle.

Because we feel that teaching self-assessment of one's fitness levels is important, we scaffold this learning by having students look at fictional fitness scores of two individuals and then compare and contrast the two fitness profiles (see form 9.15). We ask the students to then write at least two SMART fitness goals for each profile. The next step involves students assessing their own fitness scores and writing two SMART goals for their fitness profile. By analyzing data and comparing and contrasting two profiles, students are summarizing information from two stories. There are many forms of summarizing in education; in this instance, we are framing a summarization scenario by asking students to identify problems (poor fitness scores) and to come up with possible solutions by writing SMART goals. This summarization technique is called the *problem–solution frame* (Marzano, 2001).

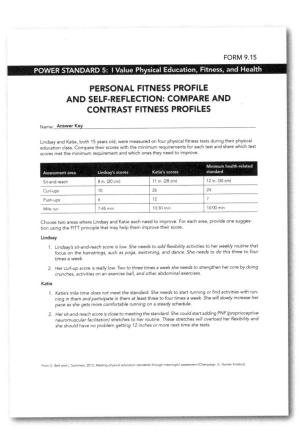

SMART Fitness Goals: Cardiorespiratory Endurance

Form 9.16 is a template for SMART fitness goals for cardiorespiratory endurance. Students fill in their fitness test scores and set goals. This assignment creates rewards for achieving and maintaining personal fitness goals.

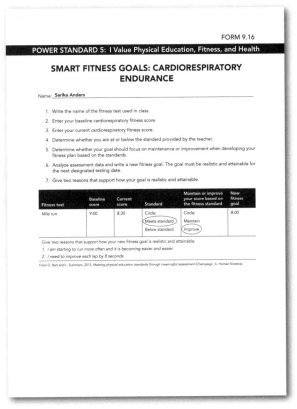

SMART Fitness Goals: Muscular Endurance

Form 9.17 is a template for SMART fitness goals for muscular endurance. Students fill in their fitness test scores and set goals.

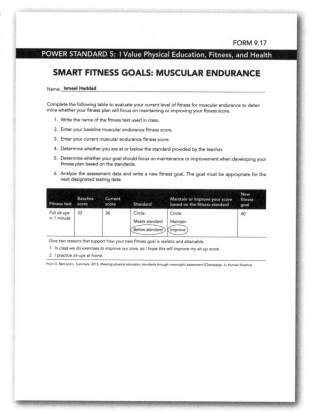

SMART Fitness Goals: Flexibility

Form 9.18 is a template for SMART fitness goals for flexibility. Students fill in their fitness test scores and set goals.

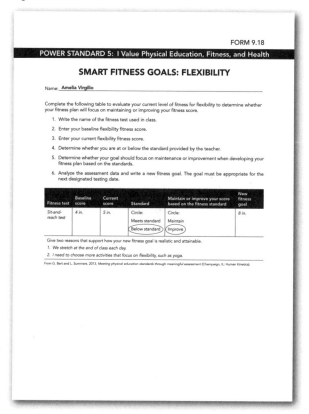

Self-Reflection Assignments

Self-reflection can also be part of our project assignments. Self-reflection is a natural consequence of recording and analyzing personal fitness data and answering questions at the end of assignments. At the end of a project assignment, it would be wise to include a self-reflective question to enable students to clarify what they mean or to express interest in physical activity. For example, at the end of the Campus Recreation Research Project, ask: What intramural sport do you think you would participate in as a college student?

We use self-reflection assignments as part of our regular written assignments. For example, we may ask at the end of a summative assessment: What do you like best about this class? How can the teacher improve this class? Improve the department? Improve as a teacher? This type of questioning gives students buy-in and a voice in the direction of the class and teaching.

Self-reflection also enables students to study their strength and weaknesses in many areas of physical activity. Keeping fitness logs and examining fitness data are some examples of self-reflective assignments in this chapter.

Fitness Calendar

Students use the template in form 9.19 to construct their own fitness calendar. This helps students learn the regularity of their participation.

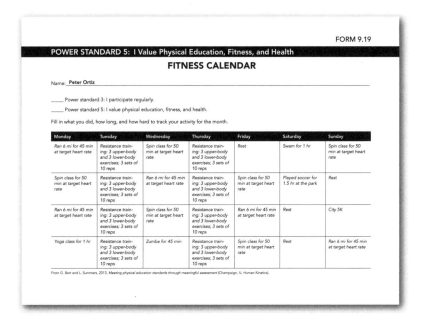

FORM 9.19

POWER STANDARD 5: I Value Physical Education, Fitness, and Health

FITNESS CALENDAR

Name: Peter Ortiz

_____ Power standard 3: I participate regularly.

_____ Power standard 5: I value physical education, fitness, and health.

Fill in what you did, how long, and how hard to track your activity for the month.

Monday	Tuesday	Wednesday	Thursday	Friday	Saturday	Sunday
Ran 6 mi for 45 min at target heart rate	Resistance training: 3 upper-body and 3 lower-body exercises; 3 sets of 10 reps	Spin class for 50 min at target heart rate	Resistance training: 3 upper-body and 3 lower-body exercises; 3 sets of 10 reps	Rest	Swam for 1 hr	Spin class for 50 min at target heart rate
Spin class for 50 min at target heart rate	Resistance training: 3 upper-body and 3 lower-body exercises; 3 sets of 10 reps	Ran 6 mi for 45 min at target heart rate	Resistance training: 3 upper-body and 3 lower-body exercises; 3 sets of 10 reps	Spin class for 50 min at target heart rate	Played soccer for 1.5 hr at the park	Rest
Ran 6 mi for 45 min at target heart rate	Resistance training: 3 upper-body and 3 lower-body exercises; 3 sets of 10 reps	Spin class for 50 min at target heart rate	Resistance training: 3 upper-body and 3 lower-body exercises; 3 sets of 10 reps	Ran 6 mi for 45 min at target heart rate	Rest	City 5K
Yoga class for 1 hr	Resistance training: 3 upper-body and 3 lower-body exercises; 3 sets of 10 reps	Zumba for 45 min	Resistance training: 3 upper-body and 3 lower-body exercises; 3 sets of 10 reps	Spin class for 50 min at target heart rate	Rest	Ran 6 mi for 45 min at target heart rate

From G. Bert and L. Summers, 2013, *Meeting physical education standards through meaningful assessment* (Champaign, IL: Human Kinetics).

Fitness and Health Logs

Form 9.20 is a two-week personal fitness and nutrition log used in conjunction with physical education lessons. Students track the food that they eat and their cardio, strength, and flexibility activities for two weeks. Logs can self-reward students for achieving personal fitness and physical activity goals.

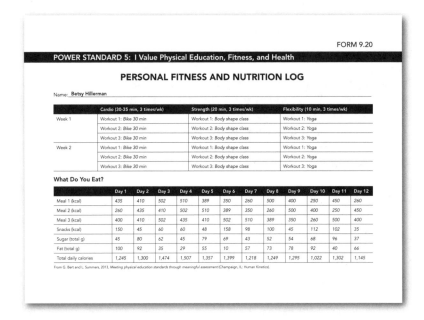

This activity directs students toward free online diet and physical activity journals such as FitDay (www.fitday.com). This is a free service and one of the best online tools available in physical education. Students can keep track of activity hours, caloric input, and caloric output; set goals; and more. We want students to learn what is available online to help support their goals and ambitions.

I Value Physical Education, Fitness, and Health: Self-Reflection

The self-reflective summative assessment shown in form 9.21 asks students how they have demonstrated meeting or exceeding power standard 6, "I value physical education, fitness, and health." Asking students to reflect on their own experiences and knowledge is a great way to assess this standard.

PART III

Getting More Out of Power Standards

CHAPTER 10

Assessing Multiple Standards

The first wealth is health.

—Ralph Waldo Emerson

The skills and knowledge that we teach in physical education are best learned as a whole or in conjunction with each other. Our brain thrives on relationships, including the relationships among the various areas of the brain and the connections among the various standards. When we assess and teach multiple physical education standards at the same time, we are putting our students into natural learning situations, allowing the brain to do its best work! We are also helping students to understand the relationships among our standards.

We do not learn skills or concepts in isolation; the brain simply does not work this way. We know that the whole-part-whole method of learning is best for physical education, meaning you should teach the entire concept, break it down into more manageable parts, and reemphasize the entire concept. Our brains thrive on making new connections with as many neurons as possible. The more connections, the more learning will take place. Individual areas of the brain were once thought to work in isolation, but research has discovered that the areas of the brain work together and connect with each other. When we isolate our physical education standards, we are depriving the brain of what it does best—integrating the various areas of the brain so that greater learning takes place.

Many of the concepts taught for each standard can easily connect with one another. In making these connections, students construct their own meaning and develop skills they will need to lead healthy and fit lives. This also allows students to see how the standards relate to each other and makes it easier for them to recall and comprehend what we are teaching and assessing. There are many natural connections and similarities among the six power standards, and often we teach several learning targets at once that are not from the same standard. For example, when we do fitness testing (standard 4: "I am fit"), we also ask which fitness concepts we are testing from (standard 2: "I can train myself").

We have provided examples of formative and summative assessments in this chapter to illustrate how you can use effective assessments when assessing multiple standards. Doing this allows us to cover all the substantial learning from a unit, quarter, or semester. This process puts learning in a more realistic setting and gives students more exposure to various standards and how the standards relate to each other.

Planning to Assess Multiple Standards

When we develop a curriculum, we often begin with a list of major concepts and processes we expect to teach. First, we present students with a specific topic (e.g., fitness plans). Upon deconstructing that topic with the teacher, students will likely discover that its component parts derive from separate standards (e.g., standards 2, 3, 4, and 6). Teachers can point out the connections and use the integration of standards as a jumping-off point for further discussion about how topics, learning targets, and standards are all interrelated. Using content and skills from several standards, we are enhancing our curriculum and encouraging students to explore a topic from a variety of angles, which helps reinforce what they have already learned.

The matrix of standards in table 10.1 shows how our tests and assessments are sufficient and representative. This table lists the summative assessments from each power standard, which we shared in part II of the book. The assessments can also assess other standards, and we placed

TABLE 10.1　Matrix of Standards

Assessments	Standard 1	Standard 2	Standard 3	Standard 4	Standard 5	Standard 6
Biomechanics of Human Movement Project	X		X		X	X
Graphic Organizer: Yoga Bingo	X		X		X	X
Graphic Organizer: Biomechanical Principle Bingo	X		X		X	X
I Can Move Correctly: Self-Reflection	X	X	X		X	X
FITT Project		X	X	X		X
I Can Train Myself and Others: Self-Reflection		X	X	X		X
Physical Activity Opportunities in My Community: Parks and Recreation			X		X	X
Physical Activity Opportunities in My Community: Fitness Industry			X		X	X
I Participate Regularly: Self-Reflection			X		X	X
I Am Fit Versus I Am Not Fit		X		X		X
Fitness Tracker			X	X		X
Fitness Log				X		X
Fitness Profile		X		X		X
I Am Fit Project		X		X		X
I Am Fit: Self-Reflection		X		X		X
Spirit of the Game Project					X	X
I Can Play Fairly: Self-Reflection					X	
Sponsoring Your Own School Run			X	X	X	X
SMART Fitness Goals: Cardiorespiratory Endurance			X	X		X
SMART Fitness Goals: Muscular Endurance			X	X		X
SMART Fitness Goals: Flexibility			X	X		X
Self-Reflection Assignments						X
Fitness Calendar			X	X		X
Personal Fitness and Nutrition Log			X	X		X
I Value Physical Education, Fitness, and Health: Self-Reflection			X	X		X

a mark next to the other standards that you can assess as well. This will help guide you when using these assessments or adapting them to fit your needs. As you become more familiar with this book and the templates provided, you will naturally see the how you can assess more than one standard.

When creating assessments from multiple standards, ask these questions:

1. Which standards and objectives do I want to assess with this test? (Every standard should be assessed in some manner, but an occasional objective may be taught without being assessed; some of the standards and objectives within this domain may be assessed through other means.)

2. Have I included questions for all the standards being tested?

3. Have I included questions that assess the critical elements of the standards?

4. Does the distribution of items across the standards reflect the importance I attached to the standards and that I communicated to my students?

5. Do I have a sufficient number of items for each standard?

Effectively assessing multiple standards might involve one or all of the following:

- Using concepts from several standards
- Creating projects and assessments that require the understanding and application of more than one standard
- Encouraging students to recognize the relationships among concepts taught from each standard
- Using thematic units that measure several learning targets for more than one standard
- Using and assessing various domains (psychomotor, cognitive, and affective)

Table 10.2 shows an example of a general rubric for any standard or learning target to assess. How do you assess more than one? You can use this particular rubric to assess the depth of concepts understood and explained, level of mastery in a skill, and the student's personal values. We highly recommend that teachers share their rubric with their students so that the students clearly understand how they are being assessed, regardless of whether the assessment is simply used to check for understanding or counts toward their cumulative grade in class.

TABLE 10.2 General Rubric

Exceeds standard (*E*)	Meets standard (*M*)	Progressing toward standard (*PRO*)	Below standard (*BLS*)
The student consistently and independently demonstrates a deeper understanding of grade-level standards and applies key knowledge, skills, and concepts beyond what is required.	The student consistently meets the grade-level standards and applies key knowledge, skills, and concepts.	The student inconsistently meets the grade-level standards. The student inconsistently applies understanding of key knowledge, skills, concepts, and processes.	The student is not meeting the standards as described and shows lack of understanding of the concepts and skills. The student is working significantly below standard in this area.
E *indicates the student grasps, applies, and extends the key concepts with more complex content.*	M *indicates the student met the expected level of performance. All students are working to be able to meet grade-level standards in all subjects.*	PRO *indicates the student is not able to regularly meet the established performance expectations or grade-level expectations for a given subject. Contact and planning with the home is important to bring performance up to grade level.*	BLS *indicates the student is struggling and shows serious misunderstanding of concepts and skills. Contact and planning with the home is important to bring performance up to grade level. Further diagnostic assessment might help determine the appropriate intervention and instructional support.*

The goal of the graphic organizer in form 10.1 is to provide an example of how to take two learning targets (from the same standard) and check the ability of students to make connections between SPORT training principles and the five fitness components. Students are asked to provide examples of how this might look, which requires them to know both of these concepts.

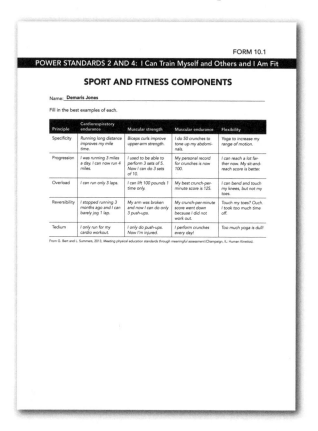

the biomechanical principles of each while also seeing the differences and similarities between these skills.

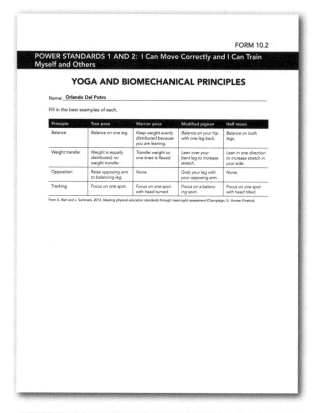

Using a graphic organizer to make connections between biomechanical principles and yoga poses is a great way to assess students' metacognition as discussed in chapter 3. Form 10.2 asks students to provide examples of how this might look. Here we have taken a learning target from standard 1 ("I can move correctly") as students perform various complex motor skills (yoga poses) while explaining the biomechanical principles used from each (standard 2, "I can train myself and others").

Again, as in form 10.2, form 10.3 uses a graphic organizer to make connections between biomechanical principles and selected sport skills Students are asked to provide several examples and compare similarities and differences. What is different from form 10.2 is that we are asking students to select several sport skills and explain

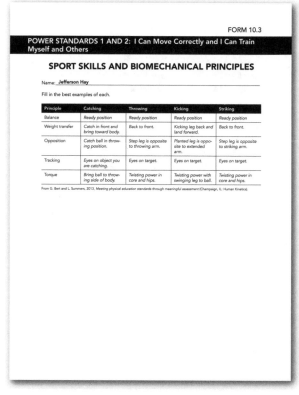

Form 10.4 is a chart that is a favorite of ours. In this activity, we ask each student or small groups of students to provide examples of how they have met or exceeded all six standards. Can students identify what we are assessing, and do they understand these standards? In the end, what they demonstrate from this assessment is that they know and are able to apply many concepts, skills, and values.

- What are the skills we have learned and are applying from many activities (standard 1)?
- What biomechanical principles do you know and can explain (standard 1)?
- What offensive and defensive strategies are you using in your games (standard 1)?
- What are the fitness components (standard 2)?
- What does your participation look like daily, weekly, and outside of school (standard 3)?
- What does fitness look like while you are playing (standard 4)?
- What are your physical strengths and weaknesses (standard 4)?
- What does SOTG look like, sound like, and feel like (standard 5)?

- Do you enjoy playing or encourage others to enjoy playing (standard 6)?

With the summative assessment shown in form 10.5, students can choose to create a yoga book that will be available in the school library, go to a local elementary or middle school and teach a yoga or Pilates class, create and record their own relaxation tape, or develop and record a yoga workout. This assessment is in collaboration with other classmates, and it assesses skills and techniques (standard 1), knowledge of concepts and principles (standard 2), and motivation of others to participate in an activity (standard 3).

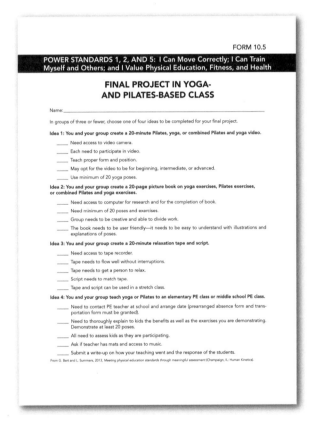

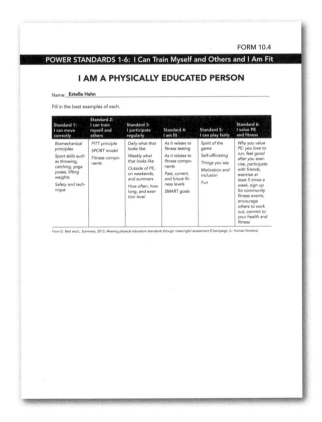

Many educators at the high school level have the privilege of teaching electives. Form 10.6 shows a summative project that we use for our elective dance class. In our elective classes, we try to create assessments based on the highest level of thinking in Bloom's taxonomy, which is having students teach others. With this assessment, students choose one of two ideas to demonstrate three standards (standards 1, 2, and 6). They can either create an instructional dance video that others will be able to be check out in the library, or they can go to a local elementary or middle school and teach a dance class. We have found that our students especially enjoy teaching the younger kids in our school district. This assessment is in collaboration with other classmates.

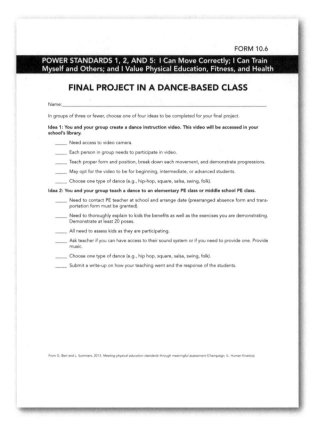

FORM 10.6

POWER STANDARDS 1, 2, AND 5: I Can Move Correctly; I Can Train Myself and Others; and I Value Physical Education, Fitness, and Health

FINAL PROJECT IN A DANCE-BASED CLASS

Name:_____

In groups of three or fewer, choose one of four ideas to be completed for your final project.

Idea 1: You and your group create a dance instruction video. This video will be accessed in your school's library.

_____ Need access to video camera.

_____ Each person in group needs to participate in video.

_____ Teach proper form and position, break down each movement, and demonstrate progressions.

_____ May opt for the video to be for beginning, intermediate, or advanced students.

_____ Choose one type of dance (e.g., hip-hop, square, salsa, swing, folk).

Idea 2: You and your group teach a dance to an elementary PE class or middle school PE class.

_____ Need to contact PE teacher at school and arrange date (prearranged absence form and transportation form must be granted).

_____ Need to thoroughly explain to kids the benefits as well as the exercises you are demonstrating. Demonstrate at least 20 poses.

_____ All need to assess kids as they are participating.

_____ Ask teacher if you can have access to their sound system or if you need to provide one. Provide music.

_____ Choose one type of dance (e.g., hip hop, square, salsa, swing, folk).

_____ Submit a write-up on how your teaching went and the response of the students.

From G. Bert and L. Summers, 2013, *Meeting physical education standards through meaningful assessment* (Champaign, IL: Human Kinetics).

CHAPTER 11

Assessment on the Run

You will never find time for anything. If you want time, you must make it.

—Charles Buxton

Time is precious in physical education, and thus it is vital that teachers and students spend as much time in activity as possible. Students learn better when they have recently engaged in aerobic activity and are using movement while learning concepts (Ratey, 2007). Fortunately, physical educators do use movement while teaching motor skills, fitness concepts, and other vital skills. What is often forgotten is that assessment does not have to always be done on paper in inactive settings, but it can be done during movement and activity. In addition, students can assess themselves and each other through movement. We need to assess while moving as much as possible so that students meet the suggested daily amount of time spent on physical activity. This approach to assessment is more enjoyable and motivating for students.

Another aspect of assessing students while moving concerns putting students into assessment games and gamelike activities (i.e., within the context of the game). Putting students into the context of the game is also called *game-based learning* (GBL). We discovered this method of teaching from the United States Tennis Association (USTA, 1998). The USTA believes that students' motivation to play tennis increases when they are allowed to play the game quickly. How many times have we been ready to teach a skill and heard, "Can't we just play?" Using small-sided games to teach skills puts students into the context of the game and fulfills their need to play

(Brown &Vaughn, 2009), which allows them to have fun. By placing students immediately into organized, structured activities, teachers also meet their need to teach to standards (motor skills), a win–win situation for all.

Game-based learning is an excellent assessment method when teachers have clearly identified what they are assessing (learning target and power standard) within the activity. For example, the teacher places students into small-sided (three-a-side) soccer games playing keep-away. While the students play, the teacher observes and assesses the biomechanics of each student using the inside-of-the-foot pass (left or right foot). The teacher records the observations using a rubric or checklist and can correct and provide immediate feedback.

In this chapter we'll share several ways of assessing students while they are actively engaged in activity.

Selecting Activities

This on-the-run assessment is an ideal method to assess power standard 6, "I value physical education, fitness, and health." It is important for students to select activities in class, because they will naturally self-select and manage their health and fitness by choosing activities that they enjoy outside of the school setting, such as health clubs, community sports, extracurricular activities, intramurals, and free play. The reasoning goes that if students are physically active in an activity of their choice (i.e., lifetime sport and fitness activities), they will enjoy the activity more. This in turn motivates them to continue with the activity because they have experienced success and enjoyment with it.

In the example shown in form 11.1, the teacher provides students with three choices of physical activity for the day: tennis, fitness walking and running, and Ultimate Frisbee. The teacher simply records the number of students engaged per activity. With this data, the teacher learns which activities students value and will most likely engage in. Teachers can also record other data such as gender preference, ability-level preference, and motor skill ability.

Students can also write a self-reflection essay on why they chose that particular activity, or they can wear a pedometer or heart rate monitor with the idea that they will reach their step goal and target heart rate zone because they are enjoying the activity.

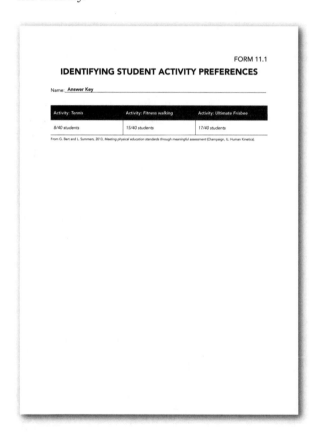

FORM 11.1

IDENTIFYING STUDENT ACTIVITY PREFERENCES

Name: Answer Key

Activity: Tennis	Activity: Fitness walking	Activity: Ultimate Frisbee
8/40 students	15/40 students	17/40 students

From G. Bert and L. Summers, 2013, Meeting physical education standards through meaningful assessment (Champaign, IL: Human Kinetics).

Voting

A simple way to assess students' attitudes, beliefs, or feelings toward any activity is having students vote with small slips of paper, stickers, sticky notes, strips of masking tape, or any other simple form of balloting. After an activity, give each student a ballot (piece of paper) and have students drop their ballots in one of two containers. For example, if students liked a fitness circuit, they drop the paper in the container with

a smiley face; if they did not like the activity, they drop the paper in the container with a sad face. Simply tabulate the votes and you now have a simple assessment of the students' enjoyment of the activity (Docheff, 2010). With indoor class activities, simply draw a T-chart on the board and place a smiley face and sad face on each side of the line. As students exit the gym, they mark their vote on the board in the appropriate column. Teachers learn a lot from their students when they simply give them a chance to provide quick feedback about an activity.

What's on the Menu Today?

We like to offer a menu of several planned activity choices for students to meet the desired learning target. By setting menus, teachers can assess student preferences of the structured activities that are provided, allowing teachers to plan offerings that meet the needs and interests of the students while still meeting the desired learning targets and power standards. This allows students to be more active because they are simply enjoying the activity that the teacher has provided.

If the goal is to improve cardiorespiratory endurance, for instance, create a menu with activities that promote cardiorespiratory health. If the goal is to compare steps per day of activities, have students wear pedometers and track their steps in several activities (in which activity did they achieve the most steps?). If the goal is to demonstrate SOTG, choose activities that allow students to demonstrate meeting this learning target.

What exactly are you assessing? Again, this depends on your learning targets and power standards. Here are some ideas of how you can use menus to assess the following power standards on the run.

STANDARD 1
I Can Move Correctly

ACTIVITY

Students select an activity from the menu. They are asked to perform skills correctly and apply tactics within the context of the game.

MENU

Field 1: Small-sided soccer: Keep-away

Field 2: Small-sided lacrosse: Required number of passes until a score attempt

Field 3: Small-sided Ultimate Frisbee: All must touch the Frisbee until a score attempt

ASSESSMENT

Teacher observes skills and tactics used or students write self-reflection responses on why they chose the activity.

STANDARD 2
I Can Train Myself and Others

ACTIVITY

Students select an activity from the menu. Students are asked to maintain target heart rate or reach a predetermined number of steps as tracked on a pedometer.

MENU

Option 1: Walk around the track

Option 2: Run the straights and walk the curves

Option 3: Run the straights and jog the curves

Option 4: Run the entire class period

ASSESSMENT

Students reach a certain number of pedometer steps, maintain target heart rate, or write a self-reflection response on why they chose the activity.

Teachers can use the template in form 11.2 to learn the number of steps students earned while playing their selected activity.

STANDARD 3
I Participate Regularly

ACTIVITY

Students select from the menu, choosing an activity that they will participate in both inside and outside of class.

MENU

Lifetime fitness: Walking, running, Nordic walking at the track

Team sport: Soccer, football, cricket, lacrosse, volleyball, Ultimate Frisbee

Racket sport: Badminton, tennis, pickleball

Alternative: Dance, skateboarding, in-line skating, bicycling

ASSESSMENT

Students fill out activity log or answer the self-reflection question, "Why do you enjoy [chosen activity]? What keeps you participating in [chosen activity]?"

STANDARD 4
I Am Fit

ACTIVITY

Students choose one of the cardiorespiratory fitness tests on the menu.

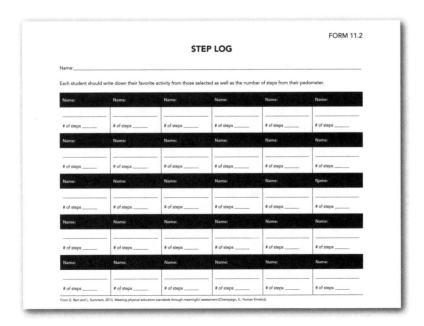

MENU

20-meter PACER test

Cooper 12-minute run or walk test

Mile test (run 1 mi [1.6 km])

Rockport Fitness Walking Test (walk 1 mi [1.6 km])

ASSESSMENT

Learning which test students prefer is an interesting assessment for both teachers and students. Asking students to choose a particular test may mean they are choosing based on their confidence and success. The goal of each test is to have students measure their current fitness level. Students have the ability to compare scores with previous tests, suggested fitness scores, and norms, and they can chart their strengths and weaknesses.

STANDARD 5
I Can Play Fairly

ACTIVITY

While engaged in an activity, students demonstrate SOTG.

MENU

Court 1: Badminton

Court 2: Pickleball

Court 3: Small-sided volleyball games

Court 4: 3v3 or 4v4 basketball

ASSESSMENT

Through observation, the teacher records examples of consistent SOTG (self-officiating, positive talk, motivation, involving everyone in play, and so on). For peer and self-observation, the teacher asks what SOTG looks like, sounds like, and feels like. The teacher provides feedback about the observations.

STANDARD 6
I Value Physical Education, Fitness, and Health

ACTIVITY

Students choose an activity from the menu, selecting the one that they most want to engage in.

MENU

Fitness activity: Intervals (walk, jog, sprint, and stride alternating 100 m for 8 laps)

Team sport: Field hockey, cricket, speedball

Racket sport: Badminton, tennis, jazzball

Outdoor activity: Nordic walking, orienteering, geocaching

ASSESSMENT

Options include teacher, peer, and self-observation; self-reflection; log or journal writing; or percentage of students participating in the activity.

Teaching Each Other

Students can be assessed while peer teaching or coaching skills and biomechanics of human movement in sport, games, and fitness activities. Students can also teach each other opposition, weight transfer, torque, follow-through, and tracking as a review for an upcoming assessment. Considering that we retain 90% of what we teach to others, peer teaching can be a valuable assessment tool for review and teaching.

After the teacher has explained each biomechanical principle, we have found that it works best to let students get into pairs. For example, in tennis, students pair up and are instructed to use the tennis racket and teach each other opposition, weight transfer, torque, follow-through, and tracking for the tennis forehand groundstroke. Students rotate the role of teacher and student. Any skill can be used; it is up to you. The biomechanics apply to all skills. The tennis ball can be

FORM 11.3

Evaluation of Peer Teaching Skill Based on Biomechanical Principles

PEER TEACHING AND COACHING

Name of student teaching: Wayne Broch

Name of student being taught/assessor: Anita Ramirez

Place an X next to the student's level of knowledge in teaching the skill of ___throwing___

Principle	Proficient and effective	Progressing and less consistent	Ineffective and inconsistent	Attempts but incorrect
Opposition	X			
Weight transfer		X		
Torque	X			
Tracking		X		
Follow-through	X			

From G. Bert and L. Summers, 2013, Meeting physical education standards through meaningful assessment (Champaign, IL: Human Kinetics).

used to teach and assess throwing, catching, and the tennis serve toss. Have students use checklists so that they can check off any biomechanics that need to be improved. These are just a few ideas of assessments that can be used. Form 11.3 is an example of a quick rubric for students who are being taught to score (according to a rubric) the ability of the peer teaching them the biomechanical principles of a particular skill.

Biomechanics Check-Off Sheets

Biomechanics can also be assessed by the teacher in the psychomotor domain. While students are engaged in an activity, the teacher rotates one group of students to be assessed on the biomechanics of a particular skill. Prepare quarter sheets that list the five biomechanical principles. This can simply be a row for each biomechanical principle with a place to put a check. For example, in tennis, students perform shadow swings (in pantomime) of the forehand groundstroke. As the students are swinging, the teacher looks at each student and places a check plus or a check minus by each biomechanical principle. Form 11.4 shows what a sheet for one student would look like without the check-offs. Once the students have been assessed, the teacher can provide immediate feedback to each student and then rotate the groups. We have six tennis courts, with four to six students to each court. The students on one court are assessed by the teacher while the others are playing tennis.

Teacher Cube Toss

On each side of a foam cube, write the name of each biomechanical principle taught. (Sportime School Specialty sells a move cube that comes with side pockets that a teacher can easily slide cards in and change what is being assessed—fitness components, biomechanical principles, training principles, food groups, essential nutrients, caloric values, and anything else teachers feel they can adapt this to. You can use this cube to help assess biomechanics. See www.schoolspecialty.com for more information on the move cube.) Students run around the perimeter of the gym while music is playing, and when the music stops, the teacher rolls the foam cube. The cube lands on one biomechanical principle, and the students pantomime the principle. This is a quick and efficient way to check for understanding of the biomechanical principles. A teacher can quickly observe the motions of the students and provide feedback. The teacher should observe correct examples of the biomechanical principle and also learn which students need to be retaught.

Student Cube Toss

Set up 10 cones along the perimeter of the gym or teaching space. Each cone should have a cube next to it. Written on each side of the cube are four of the five fitness components (strength, muscular endurance, cardiorespiratory endurance, and flexibility). In small groups (two to four students), students jog (or perform any selected locomotor movement) around the perimeter of the gym while music plays. When the music stops, each group jogs to the nearest cone, and a student in their group tosses the cube. For 15 seconds, the group of students performs an example of the fitness component that was rolled. Teachers should be able to quickly look at each group and know which fitness component was rolled because of the students' demonstration. If students are demonstrating the concept correctly, the teacher provides positive feedback. If the teacher observes incorrect examples or if a student seems confused, the teacher should go ahead and reteach that particular group or student.

FORM 11.4

POWER STANDARD 1: I Can Move Correctly

TENNIS FOREHAND GROUNDSTROKE

Name: Russell Hill

Opposition	Weight transfer	Torque	Tracking	Follow-through
Swing right, step left; swing left, step right.	Weight follows racket to gain stepping power.	Turn hips and shoulders to target, twisting toward target.	Keep your eye on the ball, contact of ball and racket, body alignment staying to the side of the ball.	Cross midline of body, racket over opposing shoulder.

From G. Bert and L. Summers, 2013, Meeting physical education standards through meaningful assessment (Champaign, IL: Human Kinetics).

Fitness Self-Assessment

Give each student an index card and a small pencil. Place self-testing fitness assessments around the gym. As students rotate on their own to each station, they perform the fitness assessment and write the score on their card. The self-tests are as follows.

Muscular Endurance and Strength

- Push-ups to exhaustion
- Sit-ups to exhaustion

Flexibility

- Sit-and-reach

Power

- Vertical jump: Tape a measuring tape on the wall, using a different color of tape every few inches. When students jump, they will see that they jumped to a certain color and can look at the color chart to learn how high they jumped. (Provide multiple stations.)

Cardiorespiratory Endurance

- Jumping rope—record highest number of jumps in a row.

Agility

- Shuttle run

Self-testing physical fitness allows students to record scores privately. Only the student and the teacher are able to look at the scores. When teachers do this regularly, students will be able to track improvement and better understand the training concepts of progression and specificity. Teachers can keep the cards and pass them out to students each time a circuit is performed.

Fitness Pit Stop

Put a cone at each corner of the regulation basketball court. The area outside of the cones is the track that students will run, jog, or walk around; this is station 1. One baseline of the basketball court has a station for push-ups to exhaustion (station 2) and the other has a station for crunches to exhaustion (station 3). Students are divided into three groups and rotate to each of the three stations twice, as directed by the teacher. This circuit can be used for students to assess push-ups to exhaustion, crunches to exhaustion, and target heart rate.

Jump Rope Relay

This relay can be used to assess fitness and sport skills. First, put students into groups of three along the sidelines of the basketball court. Two students at one sideline face the third member of their group at the opposite sideline. One of the students in the group of two has a jump rope and the third student directly across from them also has a jump rope. The students with the rope begin jumping rope with either basic or advanced jumping skills. The student without the rope runs across the gym to the person directly across from them who is jumping rope. When the runner meets this jumper, the jumper stops and hands the rope to the runner (they switch roles). This pattern continues. Decide how long this continuous relay will last. The length and distance between the groups can vary depending on the age and fitness level of your students. We like to have 20 meters or greater between jumpers, creating a 20-meter run. The assessment can be tracking students' heart rate (before, during, and after the relay). We have students take 6-second pulse readings; using their carotid artery, they count each beat and add a zero to their count, which gives the estimated heart rate. We then can question students by asking if their heart rate is at resting rate, target heart zone, or higher and how they can increase or decrease their heart rate.

Another option is simply changing the running between jumpers to a skill such as dribbling a basketball or soccer ball. The teacher can assess dribbling skills using a skills checklist. Other ball skills can also be assessed; just use your imagination. For example, to assess volleyball, place students into groups of six. Two jumpers at each end begin jumping rope. The two students who would be runners are now moving and setting a volleyball to each other as they rotate to receive jump ropes. Again, the teacher can assess setting by using a skills checklist or rubric. In this same scenario, students can throw various basketball passes to each other as they sidestep to the next jump rope station. The beauty of this assessment is that no matter what is being assessed, students are moving and reaching their target heart rate zones.

Speed Yoga

When we teach yoga, we want students to know and be able to perform a variety of poses. How do we assess students on the run with yoga? Here are some great ideas:

- Teachers call out the pose, students perform the pose, and teachers assess them using a simple rubric to check technique and form (see form 11.5). The pose lasts 15 to 30 seconds and then teachers call out another pose.

- Students work in pairs, with one student calling the pose and assessing the partner performing the pose. Students switch roles after holding the pose for 15 seconds. Supply a list of selected yoga poses for the students. A rubric or checklist is used (see form 11.6 for an example).

- Using an overhead projector, interactive whiteboard, or projector, the teacher posts a picture of a yoga pose and students write down the name of the pose and then perform it for 15 to 30 seconds. Finding pictures of yoga pictures is quite simple; magazine pages, computer images, and pictures of students can be used.

Deal a Healthy Heart

This assessment can be performed in many ways. Students can be in pairs or small groups; for each group, supply a deck of playing cards, the necessary equipment listed, and an instruction sheet (see forms 11.7-11.10). A wide variety of sports and fitness skills can be assessed. As students engage in this activity, the teacher observes fitness and skills being performed (technique and modifications). We have selected a green-friendly fitness example (no equipment necessary), a high-tech fitness example with a variety of fitness equipment, a fitness-component-themed example, and a sport-based example emphasizing sport skills. (Thanks Western Washington University for this!)

Western Washington University

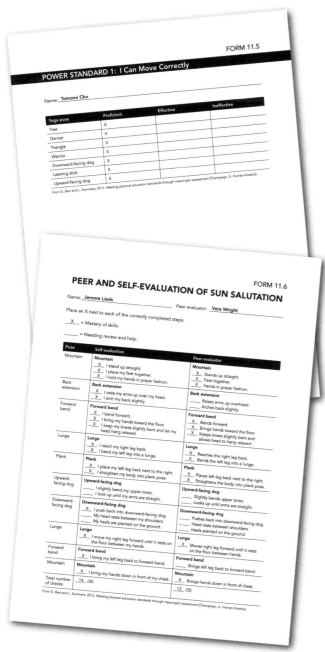

Based on information from Bellingham, WA, Physical Educators.

Based on information from Bellingham, WA, Physical Educators.

Based on information from Bellingham, WA, Physical Educators.

In Deal a Healthy Heart (forms 11.7-11.10), all members of each group deal themselves one card. Each student performs the exercises listed on the card, places the card in the completed pile, and deals a new card. When each group has gone through the entire deck of cards, the activity ends. You are assessing whether students can perform the listed exercises or skills correctly. You can provide immediate feedback and reteach techniques and skills to students who are not proficient.

Based on information from Bellingham, WA, Physical Educators.

Games

You can assess within any game you have students play. Take, for example, the game of flickerball. We emphasize SOTG and increasing success defensively and offensively. When students become familiar with the tips shown in table 11.1, we create an environment where we can assess them.

First let students play the game of flickerball (or any team sport). After about five minutes, ask students if they were successful. Then add a team rule or game restriction to increase the successes of every team member (the list gets progressively tougher):

TABLE 11.1 Flickerball Tips

Offensive tips	Defensive tips
Keep your eye on the ball.	Find a player to mark.
Get your hands prepared and ready.	Follow your mark.
Come to the ball when it is thrown to you.	Apply pressure to the player with the ball.
Be hard to guard and move to space (depth and width).	Take away the opponent's open spaces.
Communicate verbally and nonverbally.	Communicate verbally and nonverbally.

Team Rule

1. The team must make five passes before scoring. (This encourages the application of offensive and defensive tips.)

2. Coed teams must alternate boy–girl or girl–boy for five passes before a score. (This encourages communication and identifies roles and responsibilities.)

3. Everyone on the team must receive the ball before a score. (Teachers can formatively assess which students are applying each of the tips, and if they observe a student being unsuccessful, they can briefly pull the student out of the game and reteach the tip [e.g., if the student had come to the ball, the ball might not have been intercepted].)

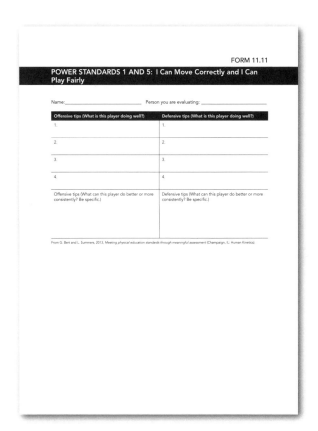

Player Evaluation

After assessing students within the context of the game, we can evaluate them using a player evaluation. Each student is given a player to evaluate for the skills and strategies that we are emphasizing, that is, the offensive and defensive tips (form 11.11).

Summary

Time is precious in physical education class. Often we have only 30 minutes once or twice a week at the elementary level and maybe a year or two at the secondary level; thus, it is imperative that we move as much as possible during what little time we have with students. With television, technology developments, and increasing use and types of social media, fewer and fewer students are physically active. In physical education class we need to maximize the time spent with our students with on-the-run activities, assessments, and teaching in order to enable optimal levels of health and fitness.

CHAPTER 12

Response to Assessment: Differentiation

Education is hanging around until you've caught on.

—Robert Lee Frost

The power of SBA is that it shows us what students are—and are not—learning. And what's the purpose of knowing what is learned? To know what needs to be taught!

Now the real work begins and the opportunity exists to be creative with our teaching. Being creative by designing alternative assignments and assessments will invigorate and motivate us to be good teachers. We can now begin working to help every student achieve and learn in our physical education classes. Teaching is more than teaching the whole class and moving on to games. After we teach the whole class, we need to differentiate our instruction to meet the needs of all students.

As we discussed in chapter 3, not all students learn at the same rate or with the same teaching methods. Differentiation is simply organizing teaching based on the individual differences of our students. It allows us to change the pace, level, or delivery method (type of instruction) of our instruction to meet the varying needs, interests, and learning styles of our students. Differentiation offers us the opportunity to reteach so that everyone may meet the standards, allowing us to plan for two situations in our physical education classes:

- What do we do with the students who have learned it (the haves)?

- What do we do with the students that have not learned it (the have-nots)?

It's important to know the 80% rule: It is time to differentiate when 80% of the students meet the standard. Once the majority of the class has met the standard, we can spend quality time with the students who have not (Jung & Guskey, 2007).

What Is Differentiation?

Differentiation is a process whereby the teacher establishes a system of strategies for students who have not learned the material and for students who are ready to move on. One may look at differentiation as simply teaching the full class, assessing the learning, and then putting students who did not learn from the whole-class instruction into groups so the teacher can reteach those who are having problems performing the game, skill, or fitness objective. For instance, in physical education this could be using an easier soccer dribble lead-up game so that those students can meet the standard. In addition, the teacher can differentiate by sending students who have performed the soccer dribble into more challenging games or drills. Simply put, teach the whole class, assess, and reteach those who have not learned.

It is important to remember that one program, teaching style, or strategy does not fit the needs of all students. It may fit most of the students in class, but not all of them. Effective teachers differentiate about 20% of the time (Hume, 2008). Teachers need to be aware of developmental levels, stages of learning (beginner, intermediate, and advanced), and students' self-efficacy (i.e., how well do students think they can perform skills?). In addition, teaching to the middle of the road or average skill level is not the best strategy because it does not reflect the skills of the highly skilled students

(Napper-Owen, 2003). Differentiation can simply be presenting students with two activities, one more difficult than the other. Another way to differentiate involves giving students choices between two or three activities (Block & Conaster, 2002).

Differentiation in physical education depends upon the following:

- Recognizing that motor skill and fitness levels are influenced by gender and growth and development

- Recognizing that students have varying fitness levels, motor ability, and past experiences with sport and games that will influence skill and fitness performance

- Assessing before differentiating

- Recognizing that students with similar needs can achieve learning goals in a variety of settings and outcomes

- Using formative assessment to decide when to move students to the next level

- Being proactive as a teacher and planning ahead; differentiation is centered on student needs

- Providing a variety of activities to keep students interested and reach as many as possible

- Increasing the creativity of our teaching so that we may provide a wide variety of experiences in order for all students to meet the standards

- Understanding that some students may need to be further challenged or work on beginning skills

- Using a variety of ways to meet skill and fitness standards

- Recognizing that students come to us with varying levels of competitiveness

- Designing assignments for students' varying levels of fitness, competitiveness, and motor ability

Levels of Differentiated Instruction

When setting up a plan for differentiation in physical education, it is useful to look at the work of Benjamin Bloom, who developed a hierarchy showing how students can meet educational objectives (see chapter 3). Bloom's taxonomy allows us to ask ourselves, how challenging should our

reteaching be? We can use Bloom's taxonomy to differentiate our teaching after we have taught the whole class. Many students will be able to move on and thus be more challenged, while other students will need reteaching and less challenging work. Bloom's taxonomy can be looked at as a hierarchy of challenge levels in physical education.

Bloom's taxonomy consists of six hierarchical levels. If we begin teaching at the most basic level, knowledge or recalling information, students can then be challenged to engage in higher levels of learning as we progress through our teaching units and Bloom's taxonomy. Bloom's taxonomy can be thought of as a differentiated hierarchy. Take a look at the following levels, which go from lower- to higher-level thinking:

1. Knowledge (know and understand): level 1 (less difficult)

2. Comprehension (explain and understand): level 2

3. Application (use what has been learned): level 3

4. Analysis (compare and contrast): level 4

5. Evaluation (assess and predict): level 5

6. Synthesis (create and use differently): level 6 (advanced)

In physical education, we use these levels to reteach or add more challenging assignments and assessments. Students may meet a standard at the teacher-selected level, or they may exceed the standard because they were able to demonstrate their abilities and knowledge at a more advanced level in the hierarchy. Remember, challenging students is not assessing the same concept repeatedly; it is giving students new and creative ways to use what they know at a higher level on Bloom's taxonomy.

Examples of Levels of Differentiation in Physical Education

Take, for instance, the physical education teacher who assigns students the task of developing a two-week personal fitness plan that encompasses the fitness components, FITT principle, and SPORT training principles. How might this objective be met when challenging students at different levels? How might the teacher use Bloom's taxonomy to adequately challenge the students?

Listed next are examples of applying the differentiation hierarchy in physical education with our two-week fitness planning assignment using the fitness components, SPORT training principles, and FITT principle.

Example 1: Personal Fitness Plan

Assignment

Students will demonstrate their knowledge of the FITT principle, SPORT training principles, and fitness components with a two-week personal fitness plan (see form 5.23).

Level 1
Knowledge: Simple recall

- Students list and define the fitness components.
- Students define *frequency*, *intensity*, *time*, and *type*.
- Students define *specificity*, *progression*, *overload*, *reversibility*, and *tedium*.

Level 2
Comprehension: Understanding

- Students give an example of frequency, intensity, time, and type for each fitness component.
- Students give an example of specificity, progression, overload, reversibility, and tedium for each fitness component.

Level 3
Application: Use the plan

- Students make a list of the exercises that they performed for one week for each fitness component.
- Students give an example of how they used each fitness component for one week.

Level 4
Analysis: Compare and contrast

- Students read two fitness plans and give five examples of how they are similar and how they are different by writing an essay, creating a list, or using a Venn diagram.

Level 5
Evaluation: Judge, critique, and choose the best

- Students analyze the two fitness plans from level 4. Which one would they select and why?
- Students may also compare the plan they chose in level 4 with another.

Level 6
Synthesis: Create, design, and value

- Students create their own fitness plan and compare it with the six power standards

for physical education. Does it meet all six standards?
- Students write a letter to the president explaining the merits of school systems adopting their plan for physical education programs.

Example 2: Basketball

Assignment

Students will have the knowledge to apply rules and will perform skills individually, with a partner, or in a small-sided basketball game with two or three players to a team.

Level 1
Knowledge: Simple recall

- Students dribble a basketball individually with the dominant hand in a straight line using correct form.

Level 2
Comprehension: Understanding and using what was learned from teacher demonstration

- Students demonstrate dribbling with left and right hands.
- Students can demonstrate chest pass, bounce pass, and overhead passes.
- Dribbling and passing can be performed individually or against another defensive player.

Level 3
Application: Use what you have learned

- Students play a basketball game with two players per team. They demonstrate passing, moving without the ball, and dribbling.
- Students play small-group games with two players per team with the ball.

Level 4
Analysis: Compare and contrast

- Students play small-group games, three players per team.
- While playing, students decide what to do with the ball after passing or catching it.
  - Pass and move to the basket.
  - Pass and set a screen away from the ball.
  - Catch and shoot.
  - Catch and dribble.

Level 5
Evaluation: Judge, critique, and choose the best

- Determine when to use man-to-man and zone offenses and defenses.

- Defense plays man or zone defense and offense must select the best offense.

Level 6

Synthesis: Create and use own basketball plays, offenses, and defenses

- Design and run various plays using man or zone defenses.
- Design and run various plays in small-group basketball games (two, three, or four per team).

Example 3: Volleyball

Assignment

Students will have the knowledge to apply rules and will perform skills in small-sided volleyball games.

Level 1

Knowledge: Simple recall, individually performing basic volleyball skills that the teacher has demonstrated

- Students demonstrate the set pass from a tossed ball.
- Students demonstrate the bump pass from a tossed ball.
- Students volley against a wall using the set and bump passes.

Level 2

Comprehension: Understanding the correct location for bump and set passes

- Students demonstrate set and bump passes in a small-group game with two or three students per side. One bounce is allowed between passes. In addition, students demonstrate the bump pass after a serve and a set pass in the front row of the volleyball court. Use unlimited hits per side.
- Students play a one-bounce volleyball game (one bounce between passes and after a serve).

Level 3

Application: Use what you have learned with regular volleyball rules and scoring

- Students play a volleyball game with two players per side, using bump and set passes only.
- Students play small-group games, two or three players per team.

Level 4

Analysis: Compare and contrast; demonstrate correct use of bump, set, and serve in a volleyball game

- Students play small-group volleyball games (two or three per side).
- While playing, students decide what to do with the ball during a volleyball game:
  ○ Pass using the set pass in the front row.
  ○ Pass using the bump pass in the back row off a serve.
  ○ Begin using the overhead serve.
- Students verbally explain the correct use of bump and set passes.

Level 5

Evaluation: Judge, critique, and choose the best

- Students determine when to use the bump pass and set pass.
- Students choose when and where to use the set pass (front row).
- Students choose when and where to use the bump pass (back row).

Level 6

Synthesis: Create and use volleyball offense or lead-up games

- Students select or create plays from a 4-2 offense.
- Students make up their own volleyball lead-up games and teach them to the class.
- Students take turns teaching bump and set skills to the class for end-of-term evaluation.

Example 4: Cardiorespiratory Endurance

Assignment

Students will maintain a target heart rate while walking or running for 12 minutes.

Level 1

Knowledge: Simple recall

- Students run for one lap and self-assess their pulse rate.
- Students record on a recording sheet what happened to their pulse rate after running one lap.
- Introduce concept of target heart rate and exercise heart rate and how to reach them.

Level 2

Comprehension: Understanding

- Students do 12-minute run or walk.
- Students record their exercise heart rate.
- What happened and why?
- Introduce the benefits of cardiorespiratory exercise.

Level 3

Application: Use what has been learned regarding the benefits and personal preferences of cardio-respiratory exercise

- Create a circuit with stations for running, stepping, and jumping rope.
- Students do the 12-minute circuit, rotating every 4 minutes.
- Ask students which activity they prefer and why.
- Introduce the concept of enjoyment of exercise and personal preferences.

Level 4

Analysis: Compare and contrast

- Students perform another 12-minute cardio circuit.
- Students check target heart rate after each rotation.
- Ask students to list the similarities and differences between the exercises. Which exercises produced the highest and lowest heart rates?
- Introduce the concept of cross-training.

Level 5

Evaluation: Judge, critique, and choose the best

- Students perform a 15-minute cross-training cardio circuit mixed with flexibility (stretching) stations.
- Again, students check pulse rates after each rotation.
- Introduce the concept of target heart rate range.
- Ask students which activities resulted in their being at the target heart rate range.

Level 6

Synthesis: Create a fitness circuit

- Students create their own cardio circuits mixed with other fitness-concept activities.
- Introduce the concepts of muscular endurance, muscular strength, and flexibility.

Example 5: Tennis Forehand Groundstroke

Use this model for any racket sport.

Assignment

Students will be able to explain and perform the tennis groundstroke.

Level 1

Knowledge: Simple recall by demonstrating skill according to teacher demonstration

- Students demonstrate forehand grip, bouncing a ball with the racket against the ground.
- Students hit the ball against a wall or fence using the forehand groundstroke grip.
- Introduce the grip (handshake grip).

Level 2

Comprehension: Understanding biomechanics of the forehand groundstroke

- Students drop and hit the ball over the net using the forehand groundstroke.
- Students swing low to high, stepping in opposition while striking the ball (low position) at waist height and following through over the opposite shoulder (high position).
- Introduce the biomechanics of the tennis forehand swing—opposition, weight transfer, torque, tracking, and follow-through.

Level 3

Application: Use what you have learned

- Students rally with another person, with or without the net, off one bounce of the ball.
- Students rally for 10 hits in a row (5 hits per side).
- Introduce boundary lines and application of force (review torque and weight transfer).

Level 4

Analysis: Compare and contrast; students perform forehand groundstroke down the line and crosscourt diagonally and understand when to use each stroke

- Students hit straight ahead, down the line.
- Students hit crosscourt on the diagonal.
- Introduce a game-based drill: Crosscourt and Down the Line. Two students rally against two other students from the baseline. One side hits diagonally across the court while the other side returns the rally down the line straight ahead.

- Introduce the margin of error of crosscourt versus straight ahead; the court is longer diagonally than it is straight ahead, and the net is lowest at the center.

Level 5

Evaluation: Judge, critique, and choose the best

- Students rally and determine their best forehand: down the line or crosscourt during a doubles game.

Level 6

Synthesis: Create

- Students create their own tennis lead-up game using the forehand.
- Advanced students help teach struggling students and help feed balls.

Using Learning Styles to Differentiate in Physical Education

Much of the literature regarding differentiation examines the use of student learning styles in the classroom. This is another category of individual differences in learning. Most of the research in this area emphasizes Howard Gardner's learning styles: visual, auditory, body-kinesthetic, and verbal-linguistic (Heacox, 2002). Students tend to strengthen their understanding through their favored learning style. Here are some examples of differentiated assessments that emphasize a particular learning style:

Visual learners learn best by seeing. It is a teaching and learning style in which ideas, concepts, data, and other information are associated with images and visual aids.

- Drawing pictures of muscles and bones
- Making a fitness calendar
- Making posters
- Forming mental pictures
- Having a keen awareness of aesthetics

Auditory learners learn best by hearing and speaking.

- Discussing similarities and differences between fitness concepts and training principles
- Listening to instructions
- Listening to prerecorded information

Body-kinesthetic learners learn best by doing. Learning takes place by the student carrying out a physical activity rather than listening to a lecture or watching a demonstration.

- Demonstrating skills to teacher or class
- Demonstrating skills during skill assessments
- Acting, dancing, or performing kinesthetic interpretations

Verbal-linguistic learners have a great ability to reason, solve problems, and learn using language. They best express themselves by speaking.

- Writing essays and other written assignments
- Doing readings
- Doing research

Consider the following examples of using learning styles to aid in differentiation.

Example 1: Fitness plan assignment (see form 5.22)

Visual learner: Create a two-week fitness calendar.

Verbal-linguistic learner: Write an essay demonstrating knowledge of fitness planning prompts.

Body-kinesthetic learner: Perform all of the prompts.

Auditory learner: Discuss or debate various workouts.

Example 2: 5K run assignment (see form 9.6)

Visual learner: Create a poster for signing up for a 5K run.

Verbal-linguistic learner: Write an essay describing the experience of a 5K run.

Body-kinesthetic learner: Provide physical evidence of running a 5K (e.g., race bib).

Auditory learner: Discuss the experience of running a 5K.

Be Creative and Flexible

Remember that teaching is all about student learning and what is best for your students. Some classes may need all six steps of Bloom's taxonomy, while others may be able to skip some steps. Physical education is not in a box; we need to be creative and teach outside the box. For instance, teaching may incorporate Bloom's taxonomy by dividing the hierarchy in two halves. When reteaching, you might use knowledge, comprehension, and application, the lowest three levels in the hierarchy, and students who have learned the material can be further challenged at the analysis, evaluation, and synthesis levels, the highest three levels. Teachers can teach the whole class and then assign the students who have mastered the material to an assignment or activity at the synthesis level. Teachers may also use all six levels or start at one level and skip another. There is a lot of flexibility in the hierarchy—it is just a guide, not necessarily a step-by-step model (although step-by-step is okay, too!). Be flexible and creative. Try it, and if it doesn't work, then experiment. Use the steps that work best for your students.

Flexible groupings of students allow teachers to vary their instruction and provide the opportunity for reteaching. Flexible groupings take into account the advanced students as well as students who need basic skill and fitness remediation. This is the essence of differentiation—teach, assess, and put into groups for reteaching or more advanced work while having the flexibility to move students in and out of groups according to their unique needs. Tiered assignments (scaffolding) enable students to progress from basic to more challenging physical education experiences. Students who need reteaching can also progress from easier to more difficult experiences—remember that students who need reteaching need more repetition and challenge, too. Challenge is for everyone!

Whole-class demonstrations and explanations are a great way to begin units of instruction, followed by ongoing assessment and groupings according to skill level, fitness level, challenge level, and reteaching needs. An example of differentiating and offering tiered assignments is putting students into flexible groups in a cardiorespiratory fitness activity and having students progress from one group to another.

Group 1: Students spend the class running as many laps as possible to work on speed and endurance.

Group A: Students spend the class running the straights and walking the curves of the track to train for the mile run without stopping.

Group Stars: Students do fitness walking to increase cardiorespiratory endurance and be able to run one lap around the track without stopping.

Notice in this example that we disguise the ability of the groupings. We call the groups *1*, *A*, and *Stars*. In the grand scheme of things, all of the students will be running and walking at the same time, so groupings by ability can be invisible. Another way to ease the stress of being put into ability groups is posting groups by student ID number or some other anonymous or less obvious identification. Of course, the teacher may also give the students a choice. Teach your students to self-select activities according to their fitness, skill, or competitiveness. With self-selecting the teacher does not run the risk of making group selection too obvious.

The following are examples of reteaching and differentiation strategies that pertain to physical education. In each category there are examples of strategies for reteaching or providing more challenging options for students. Try these ideas and experiment. Often students like it when teachers change up their teaching strategies; this adds variety and makes learning a novel experience.

1. **Class groupings.** Long gone are the days where captains pick teams and groups in physical education. Pairing and grouping students can be effective in differentiating needs and abilities to meet standards and learning targets. Here are some ideas:

- Whole class—The class participates in the activity as one large group.
- Small groups—Put students into groups of three or four.
- Small-group games—Put students in teams of three or four in competitive situations.
- Partners—Put students in groups of two.
- Have students do individual practice.

2. **Time.** You can base the activity duration, rotation, or rules on student abilities in order to increase success. Some students and groupings may need the following adaptations for time:

- Clock or no clock
- Continuous game
- Passing within three seconds; not holding ball for too long

3. **Difficulty.** Not all students will have the same readiness for one prescribed activity. Providing and recommending choices helps students who are struggling or who need to be challenged.

Here are some ideas:

- Straight line, no defense
- Zigzag; change of direction
- Against a defense
- Three, four, or five per group without a defense practicing team execution; offense
- Progressively adding offensive and defensive players depending upon the game; 3v2 defenders, 4v3 defenders, 5v4 defenders team execution; offense

4. **Space.** Space can make drills or small-sided games easier or more difficult. What we don't want to create is an environment where students are not successful because the activities involve too much space for the players to develop the skill at a slower pace and have time to make decisions. We also don't want a space that is too small to challenge students and to allow them to increase their speed of play. Here are some ideas to help differentiate with space:

- Keeping 3 feet (1 m) between offensive player and defender
- Increasing space
- Decreasing space
- Using larger or smaller space depending on groupings

5. **Special rules.** Adapting rules can increase success, participation, and enjoyment. We rarely play by the exact rules of each sport; instead, we modify them to make the activity safer and more age appropriate and to increase the number of successful participants. Here are just a few ideas:

- Use the rule of three—3 feet (1 m) away, pass within three seconds, take three steps.
- No dribble; passing only.
- Play one-bounce volleyball.
- Require a certain number of passes before a shot or goal attempt.
- Play with or without defense.
- Everyone must pass or catch the ball before scoring.

6. **Special use of equipment.** Use or modify equipment to meet specific needs. Depending on the game or skill level, the teacher can select equipment for the students' needs. A balloon is much easier to strike than a tennis ball, for instance, and a scarf is much easier to juggle than clubs. Give your students access to equipment that fits their needs, providing some equipment that is easier and some that is more challenging.

- Shorter baskets
- No goals or goalie
- Small goal target
- Restricted bounce balls
- Multiple bounces of balls in a one-bounce or no-bounce sport
- Points awarded for consecutive or number of passes

Novelty, Variety, and Choice

Differentiation does not always have to be determined by skill ability, fitness levels, or competitiveness. Another way to differentiate instruction is by offering new activities in your unit or curriculum. Changing activities and warm-ups also stimulates learning. In addition, variety in what we offer and how we deliver physical education appears to decrease stress levels in students and improve long-term memory. Here are some stress busters in physical education:

- Field day—Students choose from a pre-selected menu of activities for the day, such as soccer, lacrosse, Ultimate Frisbee, and walking or running the track.
- Keep personal fitness scores private; students take their data home and use a fitness calculator to check their progress.
- Do not grade fitness and motor skills ability.
- Change warm-up routines.
- Post on the wall the activity for the day.
- Teach something you have not taught before, such as golf, dance, tennis, or juggling.
- Dance! If you do not teach dance, learn—kids love it.
- Students select their competition level: expert, college, or rookie. Offer one field or court for each of the three levels.
- Find out about outdoor education and try fitness walking, Nordic walking, and orienteering.
- Find a local fisherperson who can teach your students fly-fishing. Look up grants for the equipment or ask for equipment donations.

- Teach yoga or relaxation stretching.
- Allow students to select workout partners when performing track, running, or weightlifting activities.
- Change it up with alternative activities and noncompetitive games such as Hacky Sack, skateboarding, street surfing, swing dancing, Pilates, yoga, stretching with bands, and whatever other ideas you come up with.
- Visit your local fitness club and look at its schedule to find some new activities that you can offer. Chances are, many of your students are already doing these activities: spin cycling, swimming, self-defense, aerobic weight training to music, circuit training, and so on.
- Bring in guests from local fitness clubs to demonstrate some new fitness activities.

Challenging High-Level Students

Talented students prefer to be grouped with students of similar ability (Morley, 2008). High-ability students are challenged and grow better when mixed with students with similar abilities. Often, when highly skilled students are put into mixed ability groups, they become bored; learning is decreased because of the lack of rigor and motivation. In addition, with mixed ability levels, there is a tendency to teach the class toward the mean or average student. Although this can be effective for beginning and intermediate students, it presents problems for the highly skilled. Average students benefit most from mixed ability groupings and the highly skilled benefit most from homogenous, high-skilled groups (Freeman, 1998).

There are some benefits to mixing highly skilled students with beginning and intermediate students. When highly skilled students serve as peer teachers or tutors, the social benefits increase. Self-esteem, self-confidence, and relating to others are enhanced through this role of peer teacher. The basic rule is use highly skilled students to assist the teacher, but do not overuse this strategy. Although this role helps the social skills of the highly skilled students, their physical skills can be compromised (Morley, 2008). Time spent with similarly skilled peers is necessary for them to grow and further develop their skills.

Here are some ideas to use with highly skilled students when they are grouped together:

- **Space.** Manipulate the space in which to play. For example, to stimulate more movement with or without the ball, a 3v3 game of soccer can be used in a large space such as half a soccer field. In other games, the space may be decreased in order to increase the challenge, such as very close tennis volleys, 2 feet (60 cm) from the net.
- **Role.** Give highly skilled students the role of peer tutor, leader, or evaluator. This has great social benefits as the students may be able to teach in a way that their peers better understand. The highly skilled students may share with the teacher how they taught the information.
- **Teaching style.** Oftentimes highly skilled students will respond to lessons with a high degree of self-discovery via activity. For example, students can study Newton's laws and how they affect certain sports and biomechanics.
- **Response.** Shape how students respond to lesson objectives. For example, the teacher may enhance learning by using highly skilled students as the demonstrators. Teachers may also receive quality feedback and assessment of teaching through student dialogue, discussions, and projects dealing with analysis of performance. High-level thinking on Bloom's taxonomy is the key here. Emphasize the top three levels: analysis (compare and contrast), evaluation (assess and predict), and synthesis (create and use differently).
- **Special rules and situations.** With highly skilled students, the teacher has many opportunities to increase the challenge and motivation by creating special rules or putting students into a variety of game situations. For example, you could take away the use of the dribble in basketball to work on passing, require students to set three screens before taking a shot to emphasize screening technique in basketball, require a bump set and spike in volleyball, or require a certain number of passes before a shot or goal is attempted in many field sports.
- **Feedback.** Make a plan for students to formulate various methods to assess themselves and their less skilled peers.
- **Challenge level.** Physical education students need to be in a stress-free environment and be challenged at the level appropriate for their skill and fitness, experience, growth, and development. Comfortable yet challenged is the key!
- **Pace.** Increase the pace of the unit. Highly skilled students will progress through a series

of skills at a faster rate. Remember that if the pace of the lessons or unit is too slow, boredom and lack of motivation may occur.

- **Learning outcomes.** Here are some special objectives for highly skilled students:
  - ◦ Understand the use of periodization in training methods.
  - ◦ Create a game using principles of space, mobility, and time (synthesis).
  - ◦ Use skills from a past lesson in unfamiliar situations.
  - ◦ Key into skills and games that demand precision, control, and speed.

- **Leadership and social responsibility.** Have students demonstrate leadership and social responsibility in a variety of situations and settings.

- **Teaching others.** Send students to other physical education classes and schools to teach skills.

Summary

Differentiation is the practice of modifying instruction, materials, content, student projects and products, and assessments in order to meet the learning needs of students. In a differentiated classroom, teachers recognize that students are different and require varied teaching methods to be successful. Differentiation in physical education keeps in mind students' learning styles, levels of higher thinking, abilities, modifications, groupings, and planned activities so that each individual can be successful at meeting and exceeding standards.

Differentiation makes us all better teachers and shows the validity of our up-to-date, research-based teaching strategies. With differentiation, the teacher will be going the extra mile and doing more than what is expected in today's educational climate. In sum, differentiation is all about student learning and helping our students become better and better.

EPILOGUE

Our goal with this book is to help guide physical educators with several research-based and teacher-tried methods in standards-based grading and effective teaching strategies. SBA is part of the complex process of teaching and learning. This process includes

1. having quality content and performance standards;

2. effectively designing teaching units and lesson plans;

3. effectively delivering teaching units and lessons in a way that engages students in learning;

4. using quality assessments (final exams, culminating performance assessments) that accurately measure student thinking, understanding, and performance;

5. using a standards-based grading system that clearly communicates what a student has learned and is able to do;

6. using effective teaching strategies, including differentiation of teaching to fit the needs of and challenge all students; and

7. having effective teacher training, professional development, and teacher accountability systems for all of the above.

Looking at this list, it is clear that SBA is part of the whole process that leads to excellence in teaching and learning. All parts of the puzzle must be in place, and this book encourages all of us to intentionally use all of these parts in our teaching practices.

The greatest characteristic of SBA is that it refocuses everything about a classroom on what's important: learning, not racking up points so a certain letter can be next to students' names on a piece of paper they get every so often. And it doesn't just refocus the students; it also refocuses instruction on student learning.

It just makes sense. If teachers want students to focus on learning (what they don't know, what they do know, and how can they know what they don't know), they must design learning experiences and activities that help students do just that.

We hope that we have inspired you with several ideas that you will implement to improve teaching, learning, and grading. In fitness, physical education, and health, we wish you well on your challenge in developing physically educated students!

REFERENCES

Alexander, P.A. (1984). Training analogical reasoning skills in the gifted. *Roeper Review*, *6*(4), 191-193.

Alsot, A.E., & Kang, M. (2010). Effects of behavior analysis interventions on skill acquisition: A meta-analysis. *Research Quarterly for Exercise and Sport*, *81*(Supplement 1), xvIII-XX.

American Alliance for Health, Physical Education, Recreation and Dance (AAHPERD). (2009). *Appropriate instructional practice guidelines, K-12: A side-by-side comparison.* www.aahperd.org/naspe/standards/nationalGuidelines/upload/Appropriate-Practices-grid.pdf.

American Alliance for Health, Physical Education, Recreation and Dance (AAHPERD). (2008.) *Comprehensive school physical activity policy continuum.* Reston, VA: Author.

American Alliance for Health, Physical Education, Recreation and Dance (AAHPERD). (2004). *Opportunity to learn standards for high school physical education.* Reston, VA: Author.

American Alliance for Health, Physical Education, Recreation and Dance (AAHPERD). (2003). *Appropriate practices for high school physical education.* Reston, VA: Author.

American Alliance for Health, Physical Education, Recreation and Dance (AAHPERD). (2001). *National physical education standards in action.* Reston, VA: Author.

Anderson, J.R., Reder, L.M., & Simon, H.A. (1997). *Applications and misapplications of cognitive psychology to mathematics education.* Unpublished manuscript, Carnegie Mellon University, Pittsburgh, PA.

Anderson, V., & Hidi, S. (1988). Teaching students to summarize. *Educational Leadership, 46*, 26-28.

Aubusson, P., Foswill, S., Barr, R., & Perkovic, L. (1997). What happens when students do simulation-role-play in science? *Research in Science Education*, *27*(4), 565-579.

Baddeley, A. (1998). *Human memory theory.* Needham Heights, MA: Allyn & Bacon.

Bangert-Drowns, R.L., & Kulik, J.A. (1991). The instructional effect of feedback in test-like events. Reported in R.J. Marzano's *The Art and Science of Teaching.* Alexandria, VA: ASCD, 2007.

Bangert-Drowns, R.L., Kulik, C.C., & Kulik, J.A. (1991). Effects of frequent classroom testing. *Journal of Educational Research*, *85*(2), 89-99.

Bauman, A. (2004b). Updating the evidence that physical activity is good for health: An epidemiological review 2000-2003. *Journal of Science and Medicine in Sport, 7*(1), 6-19.

Berk, R. (2003). *Professors are from Mars, students are from Snickers*. pp. 48-52. Sterling, VA: Stylus Publishing, LLC.

Bert, G. (2010). Teaching high school physical education according to national standards: The 6 verbs of success—demonstrate, understand, participate, achieve, exhibit and value. *Strategies*, *23*(4), 28-31.

Bert, G. (2008). Teaching biomechanics in secondary physical education. *Washington AAHPERD Fall Journal.* 36-38.

Bjork, R.A. (1994). Memory and metamemory considerations in the training of human beings. In J. Metcalfe & A.P. Shimamura (Eds.), *Metacognition: Knowing about knowing* (pp. 185-205). Cambridge, MA: MIT Press.

Black, P., & William, D. (2001). *Inside the black box.* London: King's College London School of Education.

Block, E., & Conaster, P. (2002). Adapted education aquatics and inclusion. *Journal of Physical Education, Recreation & Dance*, *73*(5), 31-34.

Borst, E.M. (2004). *Testimony to U.S. House Committee on Government Reform.* Undersecretary, Food, Nutrition and Consumer Services, United States Department of Agriculture.

Bouchard, C. (1993a). Heredity and health-related fitness. *President's Council on Physical Fitness and Sport Research Journal*, *1*(8), 1-8.

Bouchard, C. (1993b). *Physical activity, fitness, and health.* Champaign, IL: Human Kinetics.

Bouchard, C., et al. (1999). Heredity and health-related fitness. In C.B. Corbin & R.P. Pangrazi (Eds.), *Toward a better understanding of physical fitness and activity* (pp. 11-20). Scottsdale, AZ: Holcomb Hathaway.

Bouchard, C., et al. (1992). Genetics of aerobic and anaerobic performances. *Exercise and Sport Sciences Reviews, 20*, 27-58.

Bransford, J., Brown, A., & Cocking, R., (2000). *How people learn: Brain, mind, experience, and school.* Washington, DC: National Academies Press.

Brown, S., & Vaughn, C. (2009). *Play: How it shapes the brain, opens the imagination, and invigorates the soul.* New York: Penguin.

Brualdi, A.C. (1998). Practical assessment. *Research & Evaluation, 6*(6), 1-4.

Buck, M. (2002). *Assessment series: Assessing heart rate in physical education.* Washington, DC: NASPE.

Centers for Disease Control and Prevention(CDC). 2012. *Youth physical activity guidelines toolkit, ages 6-17.*

Centers for Disease Control and Prevention (CDC). 2011. *Benefits of exercise.*

Centers for Disease Control and Prevention (CDC). 2010. *How much physical activity do you need?*

Centers for Disease Control and Prevention (CDC). 2008. *Physical activity guidelines for Americans: Fact sheet for health professionals on physical activity guidelines.*

Centers for Disease Control and Prevention (CDC). 2003-2006. *Obesity.*

Chang, K., Chen, I., & Sung, Y. (2002), The effect of concept mapping to enhance test comprehension and summarization. *Journal of Experimental Education* 71(1), 5-23.

Chen, Z. (1996). Children's analogical problem solving: The effects of superficial, structural, and procedural similarities. *Journal of Experimental Child Psychology, 62*(3), 410-431.

Clarke, H.H. (1971). *Physical motor tests in the Medford Boy's growth study.* Englewood Cliffs, NJ: Prentice Hall.

Clarke, S. (2005). *Formative assessment in the secondary classroom.* Alexandria, VA: ASCD.

Clumpner, R.E. (2003). *Sport progressions.* Champaign, IL: Human Kinetics.

Coker, C.A. (2010). Practice schedules and putting distance accuracy. *Research Journal for Exercise and Sport, 81*(Supplement 1), A36-A37.

Crossman, E.R., (1959). A theory of the acquisition of speed-skill. *Ergonomics, 2,* 153-166.

Dale, Edgar (1969). *Audio-visual methods in teaching,* (3rd ed.). New York: Holt Rinehart, & Winston, pg 42.

Dempster, F.N. (1997). *Using tests to promote classroom learning.* Westport, CT: Greenwood Press.

Dempster, F.N., & Perkins, P.G. (1993). Revitalizing classroom assessment: Using tests to promote learning. *Journal of Instructional Psychology, 20,* 197-203

Donovan, J.J., & Radosevich, D.J. (1999). A meta-analytic review of the distribution of practice effect: Now you see it, now you don't. *Journal of Applied Psychology, 84,* 795-805.

Doolittle, S., & Fay, T. (2002). *Assessment series: Authentic assessment of physical activity for high school students.* Washington, DC: NASPE.

Docheff, D.M. (2010). Assessment: Trash it!, *Journal of Physical Education Recreation and Dance, 1*(81), 12-13, 56.

Doherty, R., William, R., Hilberg, S., Pinal, A., and Tharp, R.G. (2003). Five standards and student achievement. *NABE Journal of Research and Practice 1 (1),* 1-24.

Doyon, J., & Benali, H. (2005). Reorganization and plasticity in the adult brain during learning of motor skills. *Current Opinion in Neurobiology, 15*(2), 161-167.

Druyan, S. (1997). Effects of the kinesthetic conflict on promoting scientific reasoning. *Journal of Research in Science Teaching, 34*(10), 1083-1099.

Ellis, E., Larkin, M., & Worthington, L. *Executive summary of the research synthesis on effective teaching principles and the design of quality to tools for educators.* Tuscaloosa, AL: University of Alabama.

Ellis, K. (1993). *Teacher questioning behavior and student learning: What research says to teachers.* Paper presented at the *1993 Convention of the Western States Communication Association,* Albuquerque, NM.

Ernst, M., Pangrazi, R., & Corbin, C. (1998). Physical education: Making a transition toward Activity. *Journal of Physical Education, Recreation and Dance, 69*(9), 29-32.

Fisher, D., & Frey, N. (2007). *An ASCD study guide for checking for understanding: Formative assessment techniques for your classroom.* Alexandria, VA: ASCD.

Flick, L. (1992). Where concepts meet precepts: Stimulating analogical thought in children. *Science and Education, 75*(2), 215-230.

Forencich, F. (2006). *Exuberant animal.* Bloomington, IN: Author House.

Forencich, F. (2003). *Play as if your life depends on it.* Seattle, WA: GoAnimal.

Foyle, H.C. (1985). The effects of preparation and practice homework on student achievement in tenth-grade American history. *Dissertation Abstracts International, 45,* 2474A.

Foyle, H.C., & Bailey, G.D. (1988). Homework experiments in social studies: Implications for teaching. *Social Education, 52*(4), 292-298.

Foyle, H., Lyman, L., Tompkins, L., Perne, S., & Foyle, D. (1990). Homework and cooperative learning: A classroom field experiment. (Tech. Report), Emporia, KS: Emporia State University. (ERIC Document Reproduction Service No. ED 350 285).

Fraser, B.J.H., Walberg, H.J., Welch, W.W., & Hattie, J.A. (1987). Synthesis of educational productivity research. *Journal of Educational Research, 11*(2), 145-252.

Freeman, J. (1998). *Educating the very able*. London: The Stationery Office.

Gall, M. (1984). Synthesis of research on teachers' questioning. *Educational Leadership*, *42*, 40-47.

Gardner, H. (1993). *Frames of mind: The theory of multiple intelligences*. New York: Basic Books.

Gentner, D., & Markman, A.B. (1994). Structural alignment in comparison: No difference without similarity. *Psychological Science*, *5*(3), 152-158.

Ghodsian, D., Bjork, R.A., & Benjamin, A.S. (1997). Evaluating training during training: Obstacles and opportunities. In M.A. Quinones & A. Ehrenstein (Eds.), *Training for a rapidly changing workplace: Applications of psychological research* (pp. 63-88). Washington, DC: American Psychological Association.

Gick, M.L., & Holyoak, K.J. (1980). Analogical problem solving. *Cognitive Psychology*, *12*, 306-355.

Gladwell, M. (2008). *Outliers: The story of success*. Boston: Little, Brown.

Glover, J.A. (1989). The "testing" phenomenon: Not gone but nearly forgotten. *Journal of Educational Psychology*, *81*, 3392-3399.

Goodway, J., Robinson, L., & Crowe, H. (2010). Gender differences in fundamental motor skill development in disadvantaged preschoolers from two geographical regions. *Research Quarterly for Exercise and Sport*, *81*(1), 17-24.

Guskey, T.R. (2006). Making high school grades meaningful. *Phi Delta Kappan*, *87*(9), 670-675.

Hamaker, C. (1986). The effects of adjunct questions on prose learning. *Review of Educational Research*, *56*, 212-242.

Hannaford, C. (1995). *Smart moves: Why learning is all not in your head*. Salt Lake City: Great River Books.

Hartman, H. (2002). *Scaffolding and cooperative learning: Human learning and instruction*. New York: City College of City University of New York.

Hastie, P.A. (2007). Physical activity opportunities before and after school. *Journal of Physical Education, Recreation and Dance*, *78*(6), 20-23.

Hay, J.G. (1985). *The biomechanics of sports techniques* (3rd ed.). Englewood Cliffs, NJ: Prentice Hall.

Haywood, K.M., & Getchell, N. (2001). *Life span motor development* (3rd ed.). Champaign, IL: Human Kinetics.

Heacox, D. (2002). *Differentiating instruction in the regular classroom*. Minneapolis: Free Spirit.

Hellison, D. (2011). Teaching personal and social responsibility through physical activity (3rd ed.). Champaign, IL: Human Kinetics.

Heritage, M., & Chen, E. (2005). Why data skills matter in school improvement. *Phi Delta Kappan*, *86*(9), 707.

Herman, J., Aschbacher, P., & Winters, L. (1996). *A handbook for student performance assessment*. Alexandria, VA: ASCD.

Hill, A. (2010). *Framingham Study*, Boston: Harvard, Massachusetts Institute of Technology—Health Sciences Division.

Hirsch, A. (2010). FIT kids: A step in the right direction. *Research Quarterly for Exercise and Sport*, *81*(1), A-53.

Hume, K. (2008). *Start where they are: Differentiating for success with the young adolescent*. Toronto, ON: Pearson Education Canada.

Hughes, M. (1997). *Lessons are for learning*. Stafford, UK: Network Educational Press.

Hyerle, D. (1996). *Visual tools for constructing knowledge*. Alexandria, VA: ASCD.

Hyland, B. (1989). Developing student's problem-solving skills. *Journal of College Science Technology*. *13*(2).

Jensen, E. (2006). *Enriching the brain*. San Francisco: Jossey-Bass.

Jensen, E. (2005). *Teaching with the brain in mind* (2nd ed.). Alexandria, VA: ASCD.

Jensen, E. (2000). *Learning with the body in mind*. Thousand Oaks, CA: Corwin Press.

Jung, L.A., & Guskey, T.R. (2007). Standard-based grading and reporting: A model for special education. *Teaching Exceptional Children*, *40*(2), 48-53.

Kaufman, F.R. (2005). *Diabesity: The obesity-diabetes epidemic that threatens America and what we must do to stop it*. New York: Bantam Books.

Lambert, L.T. (2004). *Assessment series: Standards-based assessment of student learning: A comprehensive approach*. Washington, DC: NASPE.

Lazzaro, W. (1996). *Empowering students with instructional rubrics*. Alexandria, VA: ASCD.

Lindsay, E. (2004a). *Opportunity to learn: Appropriate practices for high school physical education*. Reston, VA: AAHPERD.

Lindsay, E. (2004b). *Opportunity to learn: Appropriate practices for middle school physical education*. Reston, VA: AAHPERD.

Lindsay, E. (2000). *Opportunity to learn: Appropriate practices for elementary school physical education*. Reston, VA: AAHPERD.

Lund, J. L. (2006). *Assessment in K-12 physical education*. Washington, DC: NASPE.

Lund, J.L. (2002). *Performance-based assessment for middle and high school physical education*. Champaign, IL: Human Kinetics.

Lund, J.L. (2000). *Assessment series: Creating rubrics for physical education*. Washington, DC: NASPE.

Malina, R.M. (1978). Physical growth and maturity characteristics of young athletes. In R.P.

Markman, A.B., & Gentner, D. (1993a). Splitting the differences: A structural alignment view of similarity. *Journal of Memory and Learning*, *32*, 517-535.

Markman, A.B., & Gentner, D. (1993b). Structural alignment during similarity comparisons. *Cognitive Psychology, 25*, 431-467.

Martin, L. (1996). *Deal a healthy heart*. Bellingham, WA: Western Washington University.

Marzano, R.J. (2001). *Classroom instruction that works: Research-based strategies for increasing student achievement*. Alexandria, VA: ASCD.

McKenzie, J. (2000). *Scaffolding for success, beyond technology, questioning, research and the information-literate school community*. Bellingham, WA: FNO Press.

Medin, D., Goldstone, R.L., & Markman, A.B. (1995). Comparison and choice: Relations between similarity processes and decision processes. *Psychonomic Bulletin & Review, 2*(1), 1-19.

Medina, J. (2008). *Brain rules*. Seattle, WA: Pear Press.

Melograno, V. (1996). *Designing the physical education curriculum*. Champaign, IL: Human Kinetics.

Melograno, V., & Kelly, L.E. (2004). *Developing the physical education curriculum: An achievement-based approach*. Champaign, IL: Human Kinetics.

Mitchell, D., & Hutchinson, C.J. (2003). Using graphic organizers to develop the cognitive domain in physical education. *Journal of Physical Education, Recreation and Dance, 47*(9), 42-47.

Mohnsen, B.S. (2009). *Standards-based assessment and grading in physical education: K-12*. Champaign, IL: Human Kinetics.

Morgan, C.F., Pangrazi, R.P., & Beighle, A. (2003). Using pedometers to promote physical activity in physical education. *Journal of Physical Education, Recreation and Dance, 74*(7), 33-38.

Morgan, N., & Saxon, J. (1991). *Teaching, questioning and learning*. New York: Rutledge.

Morley, D. (2008). Differentiation: Methods and construction when providing for talented pupils in physical education. Loughborough, UK: Youth Sport Trust.

Naper-Owen, G. (2003). Individualizing your instruction as an appropriate practice. *Strategies: A Journal for Physical and Sport Educators, 16*(4), 19.

National Association for Sport and Physical Education (NASPE). (2009). *National Association for Sport and Physical Education: Appropriate instructional practice guidelines*. Reston, VA: Author.

National Training Laboratories. (1997). The learning pyramid. Bethel, ME: Holt, Rinehart and Winston Publishers.

Newell, A. & Rosenbloom, P.S.. (1981). Mechanisms of skill acquisition and the law of practice. In D.R. Anderson (Ed.), *Cognitive skills and their acquisition* (pp. 1-55). Hillsdale, NJ: Erlbaum.

Nungester, R.J., & Duchastel, P.C. (1980). Testing versus review: Effects on retention. *Journal of Educational Psychology, 74*, 18-22.

O'Connor, K. (2007). *A repair kit for grading*. Portland, OR: Assessment Training Institute.

Ogden, C.L. (2008). High body mass index for age among U.S. children and adolescents 2003-2006. *Journal of the American Medical Association, 299*, 2401-2405.

Oki, S. (2009). *Outrageous learning*. Seattle: Washington State Policy Center.

Olson, J., & Platt, J. (2000). *Teaching children and adolescents with special needs*. Englewood Cliffs, NJ: Prentice-Hall.

Pangrazi, R.P. (2000). Promoting physical activity for youth. *Journal of Science and Medicine in Sport, 3*(3), 280-286.

Pangrazi, R.P., & Beighle, A. (2010). *Dynamic physical education for elementary school children* (16th ed.). San Francisco: Benjamin Cummings.

Pangrazi, R.P., & Darst, P.W. (Eds.), *Dynamic physical education for secondary school students*. San Francisco: Benjamin Cummings.

Pangrazi, R.P., & Corbin, C.B. (1990). Age as a factor relating to physical fitness test performance. *Research Quarterly for Exercise and Sport, 61*(4), 410-414.

Pangrazi, R.P. (2007). Activity and accountability: A PowerPoint presentation at AAHPERD Northwest Region Conference 2007, Reno, NV. www. Mauikinesiology.com.

Pangrazi, R.P., & Darst, P.W. (2006). *Dynamic physical education for secondary school students* (5th ed.) . San Francisco: Benjamin Cummings.

Payne, G., & Morrow, J. (1993). Children and exercise-appropriate practices for grades K-6. Cited in *Journal of Physical Education, Recreation and Dance*, April, 2009.

Raising Children Network Limited. (2006-2010). *Being active is good for kids*. Canberra, Australia: Australian Institute of Health and Welfare.

Raitakari, O.T., Parkka, K.V.K., Taimela, R., Rasanen, L., & Vilkari, J.S.A. (1994). Effects of persistent physical activity and inactivity on coronary risk factors in children and young adults. *American Journal of Epidemiology, 140*, 195-205.

Raphael, T.E., & Kirschner, B.M. (1985). The effects of instruction in compare/contrast text structure on sixth grade students' reading comprehension and writing production. Paper presented at the annual meeting of the American Educational Research Association, Chicago.

Ratey, John J. (2008). *Spark: The revolutionary new science of exercise and the brain*. New York: Little, Brown and Company.

Ratterman, M.J., & Genter, D. (1998). More evidence for a relational shift in the development of analogy: Children's performance on a casual mapping task. *Cognitive Development, 13*(4), 453-478.

Raymond, E. (2000). *Cognitive characteristics*. Needham Heights, MA: Allyn and Bacon.

Richardson, J.T.E. (1985). The effects of retention tests upon human learning and memory: A historical review and an experimental analysis. *Educational Psychology, 5*, 85-114.

Rink, J.E. (2001). Investigating the assumptions of pedagogy. *Journal of Teaching in Physical Education, 20*(2), 112-128.

Rothkopf, E.Z., & Bloom, R.D. (1970). Effects of interpersonal interaction on the instructional value of adjunct questions in learning from written material. *Journal of Educational Psychology, 61*, 417-422.

Ross, B.H. (1987). This is like that: The use of earlier problems and the separation of similarity effects. *Journal of Experimental Psychology, 13*(4), 629-639.

Ross, J.A. (1988). Controlling variables: A meta-analysis of training studies. *Review of Educational Research, 58*(4), 405-437.

Sanders, N.M. (1966). *Classroom questions: What kinds?* New York: Harper & Row.

Santa, C.M. , Havens, L.T., & Valdes, B.J. (2004). *Project CRISS: Creating Independence Through Student-owned Strategies* (3rd ed.). Dubuque, IA: Kendall/Hunt.

Schmidt, R.A. (1975). *Motor skills*. New York: Harper & Row Publishers.

Schmidt, R. (1991). *Motor learning and performance: From principles to practice*. Champaign, IL: Human Kinetics.

Siedentop, D. (1991). *Developing teaching skills in physical education* (3rd ed.). Mountain View, CA: Mayfield.

Siedentop, D., & Tannehill, D. (2000). *Developing skills in physical education* (4th ed.). Missoula, MT: Mountain Press.

Silver, H.F., Strong, R., & Perini, M.J. (2007). *The strategic teacher: Selecting the right research-based strategy for every lesson*. Alexandria, VA: ASCD.

Singer, R.N. (1957). *Motor learning and human performance* (2nd ed.). New York: Macmillan.

Smith, A. (2002). *Accelerated learning in practice*. Stafford, UK: Network Educational Press.

Stahl, S.A., & Fairbanks, M.M. (1986). The effects of vocabulary instruction: A model-based meta-analysis. *Review of Educational Research, 56*(1), 72-110.

Sternberg, R.J. (1977). *Intelligence, information processing and analogical reasoning: The componential analysis of human abilities*. Hillsdale, N.J.: Erlbaum.

Sternberg, R.J. (1978). Toward a unified componential theory of human reasoning (Tech. Rep. No. 4). New Haven, CT.: Yale University, Department of Psychology. ERIC Document Reproduction service No. ED 154-421

Sternberg, R.J. (1979). *The development of human intelligence*. (Tech. Rep. No. 4, Cognitive Development Series). New Haven, CT: Yale University, Department of Psychology. ()ERIC Document Reproduction Service No. ED 174-658

Stiggins, R. (2009). *Classroom assessment for student learning: Doing it right, using it well*. Portland, OR: Assessment Training Institute, Inc.

Stronge, J.H. (2007). *Qualities of effective teachers*. Alexandria, VA: ASCD.

Summerford, C. (2005). *Action-packed classrooms*. San Diego: The Brain Store Inc.

Summers, L. (2007). Tumwater School District physical education power standards. Tumwater School District, Tumwater, WA.

Talama, R. (2005). Physical activity from childhood to adulthood: A 21-year tracking study. *American Journal of Preventative Medicine, 28*(3), 267-273.

Tammelin, T., Näyhä, S., Hills, A.P., & Jarvelin, M.-R. (2003). Adolescent participation in sports and adult physical activity. *Adolescent American Journal of Preventative Medicine, 24*(1), 22-28.

Thalheimer, W. (2003). *The learning effects of questions*. Retrieved from www.work-learning.org.

United States Tennis Association (USTA). (1998). The Games Based Approach to Teaching Tennis, USTA Video. Retrieved from www.USTA.com.

Thorpe, K.E. (2009). *The future costs of obesity: National and state estimates of the impact of obesity on direct health care expenses*. Washington, DC: American Public Health Association and Partners for Prevention.

Van Der Stuyf, R. (2002). *Scaffolding as a teaching strategy*. Unpublished paper.

Walberg, H.J. (1999). Productive teaching. In H.C. Wasman & H.J. Walberg (Eds.), *New directions for teaching practice and research* (pp. 75-104). Berkeley, CA: McCuthcen.

Walsh, J. (2009). *Differentiation in health and physical education*. Toronto, ON: Canadian Alliance for Health, Physical Education, Recreation and Dance.

Whipp, P. (2004). *Differentiation in outcomes-focused physical education: Pedagogical rhetoric and reality*. Paper presented at the AARE International Educational Research Conference, Melbourne, Australia.

Willis, J. (2006). *Research-based strategies to ignite student learning*. Alexandria, VA: ASCD.

Wormeli, R. (2005). *Summarization in any subject: 50 techniques to improve student learning*. Alexandria, VA: ASCD.

Yerg, B.J. (1983). Re-examining the process-product paradigm for research on teaching effectiveness in physical education. *Journal of Teaching in Physical Education, 1*, (14), 99-112.

ABOUT THE AUTHORS

Greg Bert, MA, is a physical education teacher at Black Hills High School in Olympia, Washington, and an adjunct instructor in the education department at Saint Martin's University in Lacey, Washington.

He is a national board-certified teacher in physical education of early adolescence and young adulthood. Bert has three decades of experience teaching high school and middle school physical education as well as community college and university physical education courses. Bert is a member of the American Alliance for Health, Physical Education, Recreation and Dance (AAHPERD); the National Association for Sport and Physical Education (NASPE); and the Washington Alliance for Health, Physical Education, Recreation and Dance (WAPHERD).

In 2011 Bert received the Meritorious Service Award from WAPHERD. He was also named the NASPE Northwest Regional High School Physical Education Teacher of the Year in 2007 and Washington State High School Physical Education Teacher of the Year in 2004. Bert earned his MA in physical education in 1987 from California State University at Los Angeles. He holds a BA in physical education from the University of Southern California at Los Angeles.

Bert resides in Olympia. In his free time he enjoys playing tennis, fitness training, conducting physical education research, and spending time with his family.

Lisa Summers, MA, teaches physical education at Black Hills High School in Olympia, Washington. She has more than 15 years of experience teaching physical education at the high school level.

Summers is a national board-certified teacher in physical education for early adolescence and young adulthood. She earned a BA in physical education from Western Washington University in Bellingham in 1996 and an MA in education and assessment from the University of Washington at Seattle in 2001.

In 2009 Summers received the National High School Physical Education Teacher of the Year Award. She was also named the Washington State High School Physical Education Teacher of the Year in 2007. She is a member of the American Alliance for Health, Physical Education, Recreation and Dance (AAHPERD); the National Association for Sport and Physical Education (NASPE); and the Washington Alliance for Health, Physical Education, Recreation and Dance (WAPHERD).

In her free time, Summers enjoys water skiing, playing soccer, and running. She resides in Olympia.